Rifftide

Rifftide

The Life and Opinions of
Papa Jo Jones

PAPA JO JONES

as told to ALBERT MURRAY
edited by PAUL DEVLIN
afterword by PHIL SCHAAP

University of Minnesota Press
Minneapolis
London

Published by the University of Minnesota Press
111 Third Avenue South, Suite 290
Minneapolis, MN 55401-2520
http://www.upress.umn.edu

Library of Congress Cataloging-in-Publication Data

Jones, Jo, 1911–1985.
    Rifftide : the life and opinions of Papa Jo Jones / Papa Jo Jones as told to Albert Murray ; edited by Paul Devlin ; afterword by Phil Schaap.
        p.   cm.
    Includes index.
    ISBN 978-0-8166-7300-1 (hc : alk. paper)
    ISBN 978-0-8166-7301-8 (pb : alk. paper)
    1. Jones, Jo, 1911–1985.   2. Jazz musicians—United States—Biography.   I. Murray, Albert.   II. Devlin, Paul, 1980– .   III. Title.
    ML419.J69A3   2011
    786.9'165092—dc22
    [B]   2011008394

Printed in the United States of America on acid-free paper

The University of Minnesota is an equal-opportunity educator and employer.

17 16 15 14 13 12 11   10 9 8 7 6 5 4 3 2 1

...so much in this society is...unrecorded.

—Ralph Ellison

Contents

Editor's Preface

PAUL DEVLIN

> ... and [to] that raconteur *par excellence* Jo Jones, whose
> colorful reminiscences could be edited into a statement of
> some literary as well as documentary value.
>
> —From the acknowledgments of
> Albert Murray's *Good Morning Blues*

This is an autobiography of Jo Jones (1911–1985), the legendary jazz drummer. It was told to the writer Albert Murray from 1977 to 1985. After Jones died in 1985, Murray put the tapes they had recorded aside. In 2005, Murray loaned me the tapes so that I could transcribe them and edit them into a book. In the book's Introduction, I tell the story of the remarkable life and career of Jo Jones; here I describe how the tapes were transformed into this book.

I met Albert Murray when I was an undergraduate in college. I contacted him after reading several of his books, hoping to ask a few scholarly questions, and we quickly became friends. As a twenty-one-year-old immersed in books and trying to learn about jazz, I was enthralled by Murray's wit and wisdom. His thoughts on music, literature, visual arts, anthropology, current events, and history were intriguing to a voracious young reader and energetic student. I spent many afternoons in the early 2000s driving Murray around Manhattan: picking him up from different places, doing errands, shopping with him for books at the Gotham Book Mart and the Strand Bookstore and for music at Tower Records, checking out art exhibits he wanted to see, and doing errands and food shopping for his wife, Mozelle, and daughter, Michele.

Murray was happy to share his time with me because he was a natural educator, devoted to the idea of education and glad to see a young person excited by not only his work but the same writers and musicians that he was interested in. From the get-go, the renowned jazz drummer Jo Jones was part of our discussions. *Trading Twelves: The Selected Letters of Ralph Ellison and Albert Murray* had recently been published, and I remember bringing up the letters in which Jones (whom I did not really know much about) was discussed and how I appreciated Jones's insight into art.[1] Murray enjoyed reminiscing about Jones and kept Jones's very own drumsticks on his desk.

At some point, Murray told me about the taped interviews with Jones that he recorded while doing background research for *Good Morning Blues,* Count Basie's autobiography.[2] Murray began recording interviews with Jones in 1977 and continued until 1982. They picked up again in 1985. Murray mentioned the tapes to me several times before I heard them. They acquired a sort of mythic resonance. When I did hear them, I was dazzled and highly intrigued. At some point in 2004, as Murray was revising his final novel, *The Magic Keys* (2005), he suggested that together we might try to edit the Jones tapes into a book. By this time I had finished my M.A., was working on different writing projects, was about to begin adjunct teaching, and was looking into Ph.D. programs in English. From late 2004 through early 2005, Murray mentioned the book idea to me now and again. After not discussing the book idea for some weeks, I asked him if he still planned to revisit the tapes. He said no. He had said all he had to say about Jones in his last two novels, *The Seven League Boots* (1995) and *The Magic Keys.*

Some weeks later, he reconsidered. Perhaps he sensed my

disappointment (which I tried not to show); reconsidered the tapes; reconsidered Joe States, a character he created based on Jo Jones; or some combination. After *The Magic Keys* was published in May 2005 and the publicity period for the book had passed, we planned to start working on the Jones tapes.

I had previously done some routine typing for Murray. While Murray's longtime typist Alice Adamczyck (an accomplished librarian and bibliographer) typed his major manuscripts for many years, he still had other typing he needed done (though he knew how to type himself). He dictated to me things like recommendation letters for people, short nonfiction pieces or ideas that he thought might be used later, a short story, and the essay that became "Jazz: Notes toward a Definition."[3] At first I thought that working on the Jones project was going to require more typing than thinking, but soon I discovered that I would be largely on my own, with Murray's encouragement.

We were planning to start work on the project in the summer of 2005, but problems of old age sent Murray to the hospital for almost a month. He endured a sharp physical decline and loss of physical strength that required him to spend most of his days in bed and in need of nursing care. In late August 2005 he suggested that I take the Jones tapes with me, transcribe them, bring him the transcriptions, and we'd see what we had.

LISTENING TO JONES'S VOICE

My first attempts at transcription taught me that it was not easy, and in fact it was incredibly difficult. There is a reason why court reporters are so well paid. Try playing a section of someone talking at the normal-quick pace of conversation. Wait a few moments, then type it out. Listen to the tape again. It's not quite the same. The mind often instantaneously re-arranges what it hears into an approximation of what was said so that it might be typed out quickly and easily. Transcribing anything is difficult enough, but Jones had a unique way of talking: fast, then slow; loud, then soft, then very fast; and so on. Add to that the blizzard of unfamiliar proper nouns (how do you spell *that* name?) and stories that stop, drift into something else, and then pick up again.

I spent several months just listening to the tapes, gaining a real familiarity with them, looking up people and the events they referred to, and spending countless nights falling asleep while listening to them. I developed great affection for this character on the tapes. An appealing blend of wisdom, sincerity, humor, and natural irreverence made for enthralling listening. The alternately roguish yet serious character that came through on the tapes was one I liked and one that I thought the world should have the opportunity to get to know. Also, I felt that there was something about the way his mind worked that is parallel to the way my mind works. I can't quite put my finger on it, but Jones makes mental leaps and connections (rather metonymically) in a way that I do and in a way that I find natural. I like to make jumps and connections without intervening explanatory steps, and so does Jones. Maybe, or probably, Murray recognized this early on, which is why he began to consider me for the project. I am certainly not implying any mystical connection to the mind of Jones, only pointing out that this is another way, in addition to love of the music and feeling for history, in which I clicked with the material.

While I was editing the tapes that became *Rifftide,* I was encouraged by reading other as-told-to jazz autobiographies, for example, the wonderful recollections of Garvin Bushell (*Jazz from the Beginning* as told to Mark Tucker, 1988) and Baby Dodds (*The Baby Dodds Story* as told to Larry Gara, 1959). I also read Ellington's *Music Is My Mistress* (as unofficially told to Stanley Dance, 1973).[4]

I was cheered on by the recognition that *Rifftide* is a not-so-distant cousin of these texts. I could only assume that Mark Tucker and Larry Gara must have dealt with some of the same problems that I did, such as editorial questions of how to order and arrange material. It might be worth noting in the interests of full disclosure that like Tucker and Gara and Dance, I am, ostensibly and for practical purposes, a white guy editing a black guy's story, although also like them and like Jo Jones and Albert Murray and millions more, culturally an omni-American, to use Murray's famous appellation from the title of his first book.[5] Of course, they knew their subjects personally, and I was working at a remove of one person and two decades. After a busy twenty years, and in his nineties, Murray could not recall certain details about Jones's life. Even if he knew them to begin with, a second-hand account, however good, is not the same as being able to collaborate with the subject under discussion in person. I decided that ultimately the drawbacks this presented were outweighed by the importance of getting the material down and on the record. I believe that since Jones was such a serious student of African American history, adamantly fighting on behalf of cultural memory and against our culture's pervasive amnesia (what Frank Rich has aptly called "the great American memory hole"),[6] it is fitting and appropriate that his story be published. Jones also was dedicated to the idea that exemplary lives should be carefully studied.

Murray read and/or listened to me read the entire text of *Rifftide,* mostly in 2006 and 2007, but also from 2008 to 2010. He offered some minor editorial suggestions. (Of course, any errors are mine and not his.) At times he provided supremely interesting context (for example, see the note on Roscoe Conkling Simmons in "I Often Wondered Why I Was Such a Strange Fella"). His most frequent and important admonition was to "clean it up so that we can read it but not so much that we lose the rawness of Jo's style." The goal was to find the balance between readability and fidelity to the orality of the discourse.

I transcribed nearly all of almost every tape before I started arranging and making sense of the material. I often had to do what at times felt like prodigious amounts of editing. At other times, less cleanup was needed. Much of this work was done in 2006 and 2007, but the work of transcription and editing peaked in 2009 and early 2010.

A challenge was posed for me by Murray's review essay "Louis Armstrong in His Own Words," which appeared in his 2001 essay collection *From the Briarpatch File*. The challenge involved squaring, or thinking through, certain claims Murray makes about Louis Armstrong's journal entries with the mass of material that now composes the recollections of Jo Jones.[7] I spent an inordinate amount of time thinking about the problems posed. Murray states, in the process of surveying Armstong's various autobiographies:

> As any competent student of literary composition should
> know, the more natural and casual a voice sounds in print,
> the more likely it is to have been edited time and again.
> It is not a matter of making a record of things, memories,
> opinions, and notions as they come to mind. It is a matter
> of composition. . . . If it is properly done, the "as told to"
> autobiography represents how the subject wants his story
> told. To achieve this end, he enlists a competent and em-
> pathetic craftsman to make him sound like he thinks his
> voice should come across on the page.[8]

Murray's point is that while Armstrong's published journals and diaries are interesting, and "a very significant source for the study of Louis Armstong," the "irresistibly elegant good taste that is always there in Armstrong's music is just simply not very often there in his 'writing.'"[9] Perhaps that was not the fairest way it could have been put, but Murray makes a nuanced and persuasive case. Armstrong had a certain interest in being a writer that Jones did not have at all. At the same time, Jones admired writers and writing with reverence and seriousness, substantially more so than Louis Armstrong seems to have done. (Jones seems to confirm Ralph Waldo Emerson's claim that "a master likes a master, and does not stipulate whether it be orator, artist, craftsman, or king.")[10] To sum up, Louis Armstrong's journals are historically important, often intriguing, but a little flat. Jones's discourses are a shaken seltzer bottle.

Later in his review essay, Murray praises the "fine, uninterrupted narrative" that Richard Meryman crafted in "Louis Armstrong: A Self-Portrait," which was later published as a book.[11] That is all well and good for the cooperative musician who wishes to have his story told in a straightforward, conventional way. But Jones did not answer questions in a reasonable way. Frankly, he did not seem to enjoy answering questions at all, so Murray more or less stops asking them early on. Jones just talks and talks, but I do not believe he simply presented Murray with "things, memories, opinions, and notions" as they came to mind (although he did that sometimes). From the many brief preliminary comments he starts stories with, it appears that Jones often thought about what he was going to say first.

Furthermore, the personality he put forth on his album *The Drums* (1973), revealed in his discourse with all its starts, stops, and jumps and cuts in subject matter, in which he tells stories of the important (well-known and unknown) jazz drummers and demonstrates their drumming techniques, is essentially the personality that comes across on the tapes and thus in *Rifftide*. Ralph Ellison called Jones's voice a work of art, but in a sense his whole persona was a work of art as well. There was certainly a performance taking place (keep in mind the "dramatics" and "dramatic skits" in which Jones performed early in his career). At times it seems to be something like some sort of lowercase "d" dada performance. The "Jo Jones" that appears in Nat Hentoff and Nat Shapiro's book *Hear Me Talkin' to Ya: The Story of Jazz as told by the Men Who Made It* (1955) is the same one here in this book and so is the Jo Jones that appeared in Dan Morgenstern's 1965 profile and in many interviews.[12] What appears in *Rifftide* is Jones's persona, the one that he crafted. Sometimes he could ham it up like John Barrymore in the film *Twentieth Century,* and sometimes the solemnity of his seriousness was quasi-religious, as though he were speaking as some sort of wise holy man. Everything is fluid and authentic. It's who he was. As he once said of a famous drumming colleague, he "was an all-around man." Jones knew he was creating and presenting a character—but at the same time, he really was the character. Again, I did not know him in person, so take this with a grain of salt. This is the sense that I get from thinking about this topic nonstop for some time. Long story short: Jones was too explosive, too creative, too off-the-wall to say, "I was born here, did this, that, and the other thing," and that's how I want the book to read.

Jo Jones presents a different case from Count Basie and some other musicians, even Louis Armstrong (who wrote a lot but did not seem to have read a lot), because he was more text-aware, text-oriented, text-driven. Jones was a serious reader with a large library. He was a voracious consumer of newspapers and periodicals, novels, and nineteenth-century psychological treatises. He knew what a run-of-the-mill narrative would be like, yet he makes no effort to present Murray with a rough draft of a life story that just needed editing, and Murray quickly realized that the questions required to establish the framework for such a narrative were not going to be answered in a cooperative way.[13] Jones answered questions about Basie and the Basie band, but recoiled from questions about himself. He was going to say what he wanted to say, and that was going to be the end of it. Jones is fine with Murray's interjections (which Murray does not often make), but specific questions often lead to annoyed or faux-exasperated answers. For instance, when Murray asks when Jones transitioned from mainly playing piano and trumpet to drumming, Jones replies, of drumming, "Well, I always could do *that!*"

ASSEMBLING THE BOOK

A tremendous amount of cutting, pasting, and shuffling was required to get this text into its present form. Every tape contained every topic in the seven chapters. The profiles of various people in "People I've Rubbed Elbows With" were spread out all over the tapes (in more or less full form; they were not stitched together). The largest challenge was finding ways to put like with like. I had to be creative in my arrangement of material. How would such and such section look coming after such and such a paragraph but before this other paragraph? In short, I gave a kind of order to many hours of unstructured interviews, thus making a collage out of numerous messy but compelling stories. Luckily for me, Jones tells quite a few self-contained vignettes that form crisp little paragraphs with clear beginnings and ends.

I preserved the grammar that Jones uses. Jones knew proper grammar but often chose not to use it. I did not feel it was my place to correct his mistakes. I tried to follow Murray's guidelines in cleaning it up somewhat but not so much that we lose what makes his voice special.

Jones tells some of the same anecdotes on several tapes (or in some cases, on almost every tape), and I used what I thought were the best versions. Sometimes I combined different versions of the same story. Usually the difference between versions consisted of a minor detail or perhaps a bon mot in one that was missing from the other. The stories he tells most often are about Basie and the band and Basie band business in Kansas City, as if he wants to do his best to make sure that

Murray gets the information down for Basie's book. He does not often repeat stories about himself.

Some names were changed to protect the innocent and the guilty. In one instance, a name was so garbled on the tape (and research yielded nothing) that I had to name the person "unintelligible." To whoever "unintelligible" is, I apologize. You deserve a lot of credit for putting up the monument to the great African American jockey Isaac Murphy.

The metaphorical cutting-room floor also contains other items, such as outside-the-box claims about historical public figures that Jones did not appear to know and that could not be verified. Some of these claims were comedic; some were not. In any event, I chose to keep certain material in and leave other material out. I had to use my judgment. The silly section about Sinclair Lewis (in "My Thirst after Knowledge Will Never Cease") was left in because I think the comedy translates onto the page, and the claim is so outlandish that nobody could take it seriously. Besides, Lewis wrote some of his best work after 1940. At any rate, the reputation of the truly great Sinclair Lewis will not be damaged.

Jones made some decisions easy for me by either ending or prefacing a tale by telling Murray, "This is for your private stock" or "This is private stock." On other occasions, he simply told Murray to "turn that [tape recorder] off," and he did so. With other material, I had to use my common sense and good judgment. Everything that was left out is only tangential and historically unimportant. At times Jones vents his day-to-day frustrations (and more structural frustrations) with the music business; these are similar to the frustrations that most people have with their jobs. I generally felt these moments were not worthy of inclusion in the book. There are also many stories that were just too fragmented or sketchy or unclear. Non sequiturs abound. I called one section "a blizzard of non sequiturs" but ended up fitting some of them in elsewhere and just left others out. While I have professional experience in the scholarly editing of unpublished text, I quickly found that standard accepted concepts regarding creative unfinished works on paper did not apply to a group of recordings such as these.

First and foremost, I preserved the commitments Murray made to Count Basie regarding the omission of unnecessary, private material in *Good Morning Blues* while at the same time (for the most part) allowing Jones to relate his personal perspective on Basie. Jones's Basie is not quite Basie's Basie (or Murray's Basie, depending on how you look at it). Jones's Basie, I think, enhances and nicely complements the Basie of *Good Morning Blues.* To be honest with history, Jones and Basie's friendship suffered some strain by the 1970s, and at times it seems as if Jones almost wants Murray to be a kind of ambassador between him and Basie. Indeed, in *Good Morning Blues,* the last time Basie (through Murray) mentions Jo Jones, it is not a positive mention. And yet, after the incident Basie describes (Jones leaving the band allegedly without notice in 1948), Jones did sit in with Basie's band on various occasions (such as at the Newport Jazz Festival in the 1950s), and Basie did play piano on one tune with Jones on a later recording date.[14] Jones's side of the story is that his wife's death in 1946 did not fully hit him until 1948.

Jones's various frustrations with Basie in the late 1970s take up a lot of time and tape; I have passed on just a taste of them here for the sake of history. I think that introducing this unspoken subtext, to know that they went through this long-term, incomplete semi-fallout, enriches the complexity of the text and the complexity of each man. Jones's frustrations with Basie do not take up as much tape as his affection for Basie and his fierce loyalty to him. At the same time, certain grand stories about Basie from the good old days were left out of this book. Private stock!

"He don't need me, and I don't need him," Jones says of Basie at one point, as if recognizing the cold shoulder he has been receiving, "but together, we can enhance *each other,* for *posterity.*" On this occasion Jones was frustrated because in the late 1970s Basie nixed the proposal of a jazz enthusiast from Japan who (according to Jones) offered to pay $150,000 for a new album featuring Jones playing with Basie's band. "Basie could have kept seventy-five, gave me fifty, and used twenty-five to pay off the band," Jones notes. This was not frustration born of greed. He was not yet struggling financially (though he was soon to be), but he was certainly not comfortable, and meanwhile Basie was very comfortable, perhaps even wealthy. I was reluctant to relay such information without offering Basie's side of the story (lost to history). Phil Schaap reminded me that Basie was under contract to Norman Granz and therefore could not simply go record for someone else. Also, as Schaap noted, dealing with Jones in these years required patience, which Basie had, but perhaps not enough for Jones's liking.

Murray never comments when Jones begins venting about Basie in this manner. On the final tape (July 1985), sounding audibly frail and with dramatically less snap, a very ill Jones furiously laments that Basie, who died a year earlier, did not leave him the motor scooter that he used in order to get around in his last years. (Jones delivered what many consider to be a near-miraculous performance at the memorial concert for Basie at Carnegie Hall in 1984.)[15] Murray tells Jones that he'll contact Basie's estate to try to locate the scooter and see if he can obtain it for him. (Jones died two months later.)

Murray: I think it's called "Amigo" or something like that?

Jones: I don't know what the hell it's called!

I felt a great sadness when listening to all this on the tapes and still do when thinking about it now. It is a feeling similar to the one Shakespeare seems to want the audience to feel at the end of *Henry IV, Part Two* when the erstwhile Prince Hal (now king) denies his former friend, the larger-than-life Falstaff. The analogy (with Basie as Hal and Jones as Falstaff) is not perfect for many reasons (Basie was seven years older than Jones, for instance), but in the abstract it's rather workable, especially in light of Jones's tales of Kansas City, "back when it was *lean days*."

I decided not to annotate most of the jazz-related material. At the same time, many readers already know the history of Basie's band and explaining, for example, who Lester Young was would be superfluous. At some point, in any work of nonfiction, some knowledge about some things must be assumed. In general, if basic information about something or someone was readily and easily available online in early 2010, I decided, with some exceptions, not to give it a note. Other annotations that I felt would explain and enhance the text developed out of sources such as books, documentaries, personal knowledge, or conversations (such as with Murray or Michael James). In certain instances I added Murray's reply on the tape to something Jones said or Murray's comments or riffs on the tape because I felt it enriched the text. In other instances I added an observation that came to my mind if I thought it was a good one. Sometimes I thought an unclear or obscure item would benefit from explanation. But as Jones would say, enough about that.

EDITOR'S ACKNOWLEDGMENTS

I'd like to thank Albert Murray for giving me the opportunity to edit the tapes and having faith in me to do the right thing. Any errors or mistakes in this book are mine and not his. I'd especially like to thank Mozelle (Mrs. Murray) and Michele Murray.

Thanks to Lewis P. Jones, close friend and legal representative of Albert Murray and the Murray family. Without his dedication and insight, this book would not have been possible. In addition to his many personal and professional commitments as a family man, investor, entrepreneur, board member of charitable organizations, and guardian of the Murray family's best interests, Lewis found the time to be closely involved with *Rifftide* and came up with the title.

I am indebted to Pieter Martin and Richard Morrison of the University of Minnesota Press for believing in the book. I also thank everyone else at the Press who was involved, especially Nancy Sauro and Adam Brunner.

I have many more people to thank for their assistance, and as many of those listed below are also friends of Albert Murray, he thanks them as well. Phil Schaap wrote the Afterword and shared his deep and unique knowledge with me. Our lively discussions about Jo Jones were enlightening and inspiring.

Loren Schoenberg, executive director of the National Jazz Museum in Harlem, organized a Saturday Panel on Jo Jones there in 2009 and invited me to speak. I thank Loren for that and for his keen insights and strong encouragement. On that day I was grateful to meet Benny Powell and Dick Katz, both of whom played with Jo Jones when they were starting out and, sadly, are no longer with us. I was privileged to hear their recollections.

I'm very grateful to Roy Haynes, who generously discussed his rich memories and impressions of Jo Jones with me in several fascinating conversations. Kenny Washington and Grady Tate were also kind enough to share some thoughts and anecdotes with me. Thanks to Greg Thomas for putting me in touch with these three great drummers and for his encouragement.

Many thanks to the Institute of Jazz Studies (IJS) at Rutgers University, especially its director, Dan Morgenstern, and its photograph archivist, Tad Herschorn. Tad was extraordinarily generous with his time and put an amazing effort into locating and scanning the many photos that IJS graciously allowed to be included in *Rifftide*. IJS also allowed me to do archival research, for which I am very appreciative.

Thanks to Joe Wilder, legendary trumpet player and extraordinary photographer, for allowing us to use his photo of Jo Jones. Thanks to Frank Stewart, senior staff photographer at Jazz at Lincoln Center, for allowing use of his photo of Albert Murray and Count Basie. Frank Driggs was kind enough to allow the use of the photo on the cover.

Sidney Offit, a wise man and great writer, believed strongly in *Rifftide*, and I'm grateful for his encouragement. Gary Giddins shared his thoughts on Jo Jones with me and kindly looked up pieces he'd written about Jones that I could not otherwise locate. Phoebe Jacobs of the Louis Armstrong Educational Foundation was kind enough to discuss her remarkable memories of Jo Jones with me on several occasions. Charlie Davidson read an early draft of *Rifftide*, and his enthusiasm for it was inspirational. Henry Louis Gates Jr.'s encouragement meant a lot, and his commitment to the preservation of history is inspiring. Thanks to Wynton Marsalis, from whom I have learned a great deal, and the many wonderful people involved with Jazz at Lincoln Center, especially Genevieve Stewart, Ken Druker, the Schiff family, and Gordon Davis.

Thanks to the scholars and writers I'm acquainted with who have studied Albert Murray's work: Barbara Baker, John Callahan, Lauren Walsh, Caroline Gebhard, Jeanie Thompson, Roberta Maguire, Robert O'Meally, Herman Beavers, Roy Hoffman, Ravi Howard, and Kern Jackson. Thanks to Philip Clark and his family. Thanks to Jay Lamar, Director of the Caroline Marshall Draughon Center for the Arts and Humanities at Auburn University, for her and the Draughon Center's commitment to the study of Albert Murray's work. And thanks to Jay for her encouragement regarding *Rifftide*. Thanks to Dana Chandler at Tuskegee University. Thanks to Thomas Litland for his assistance and encouragement.

At Stony Brook University, thanks to Susan Scheckel, Jeffrey Santa Ana, Rowan Ricardo Phillips, Roger Rosenblatt,

Celia Marshik, Stephen Spector, Ed Casey, Krin Gabbard, Wilbur Farley, Matt Gilbert, Laurence Zellner, Patrina Jones, and Rachel Hartman. At St. John's University, thanks to Granville Ganter, Stephen Sicari, Greg Maertz, John Lowney, Steve Mentz, Dohra Ahmad, Eugenia Smilowitz, Tara Roeder, and Kevin Kennedy.

Thanks to my family: my mom, Rosemary Devlin; my dad, James Devlin; my sister, Tara Devlin; Maureen Tracy, Patricia Tracy, Kathy and Tony Millon, Bill and Carolyn Tracy, and all the Millons, Tracys, Borgias, and Devlins. Thanks to the following friends: Naomi Caesar, Justin Benjamin, Russell Relethford, Peter Cooper, Ernest Scalamandre, Duke Barnett, John Colgate, Stuart Katzoff, Thomas Bostwick, Nick Paumgarten, and Peter Dagher.

Last but certainly not least, I must thank Michael James (1942–2007). Mike was Duke Ellington's nephew and a very close friend of both Jo Jones and Albert Murray. Mike and I spent many hours talking about Jo Jones, and he perused some of the earliest transcripts I created for *Rifftide*. Mike and Papa Jo would occasionally go to see Philly Joe Jones perform. Mike said that when they'd be sitting on the side of the stage, or backstage, Papa Jo would notice Philly Joe's quotation of the history of drumming in his drumming vocabulary. For instance, Jo would say to Mike, while Philly Joe was playing, "Shadow is on the stage," meaning Philly Joe was playing something that brought Shadow Wilson to mind. "Max is on the stage," he'd say, when a Max Roach–inspired moment occurred. "And there I am!" Papa Jo would add when he saw his influence. The vast amount of information Mike shared with me was all crucial and indispensable for me to hear, and I can't thank Mike enough for taking the time to explain the depth and complexity of Jo Jones. Extra special thanks to anyone I may have inadvertently forgotten.

Introduction
The Musical Life of Papa Jo Jones

PAUL DEVLIN

> I first saw Jo Jones at the Roxy Theater in 1944, just
> before he went into the Army. His personality filled the
> great New York movie palace. Backing a line of thirty-
> six girls and a variety of acts, catching every nuance, he
> swung like mad, making it all seem easy as pie. "If you
> were there, you really heard me," Jones said. "I carried
> two bands—Paul Ash's and Basie's."
>
> —Burt Korall, *Drummin' Men*

JO JONES: HIS LIFE AND MUSIC

Jonathan David Samuel Jones—save your breath, "Jo"—has
more often than not been called the greatest drummer in the
history of jazz. Most great jazz drummers have given testi-
monials to Jones's virtuosity and innovation. This book is his
story, derived from interviews with Albert Murray and transcribed, edited, and arranged by me. Jones stood out as larger
than life in a world of large personalities. He was a raconteur
and tall-tale spinner. His unusual style of narration, combined
with his involvement in important moments in musical and
cultural history, and along with his observations about other
intriguing figures, have resulted in this autobiography. It is
not *the* autobiography but it is *an* autobiography of Jo Jones.

1

Jones seemed to have had a propulsive force in his personality, a magic ingredient that amplified inventiveness, irreverence, originality, and—for lack of a better term—general fabulousness and outrageousness. He was a ribald comedian, an experimental storyteller, and a moral philosopher—not necessarily in that order. There was a something, some spark, that creates the sense of an infinite and uncontrollable yet nimble mind, something approaching the absolute sublimity of some of Shakespeare's larger-than-life characters. I did not get a chance to meet him. I have discussed him with many people who knew him well, and I spent years immersed in the tapes of his discourses that are the basis for this book.

Jo Jones was a man of tremendous scope who experienced both the heights of stardom and the depths of personal tragedy several times over. He was born in Chicago on October 7, 1911, to Samuel and Elizabeth Jones. Against the flow of the Great Migration, the family headed south to Alabama. Samuel Jones was an electrician, boatbuilder, and industrial engineer. On July 17, 1922, Samuel Jones was killed in an accident while trying to repair a piece of machinery.[1] The machine killed him when it broke apart. This devastating event led young Jo Jones, by 1923, directly into the world where he would spend the rest of his life: show business. He loved and always used the term "show business" though he became a fine artist without parallel. Eleven-year-old Jones entered a world that in some ways must have been more like the nineteenth century than the twentieth: the wild world of carnivals, traveling circuses, Chautauqua circuit shows, and medicine shows. He did this in order to help support his mother and his sister, Lillian.

The death of his father was not Jo's first taste of adversity. Some years prior, while Samuel Jones was still alive, Jo was badly burned by attempting to light a cigar with a newspaper in imitation of an uncle. The burns he received left him an invalid for eighteen months. He would later say, "The whole thing taught me understanding. Having had a real bad experience, young, made me the way I am."[2] There are certain interesting parallels between Jo's experience and that of the novelist Saul Bellow (1915–2005), who also spent a large amount of time as an invalid as a child. Both became voracious readers and tireless artists and became famous for being exceptionally energetic and alert later in life.

When Jones hit the road as an entertainer—musician, actor, comedian, dancer—it was not a permanent abandonment of home. Perhaps he worked as a performer as a sort of summer job or occasional job because he attended junior high school and at least some high school in Alabama and later the A&M Institute in Huntsville, a junior college then, now Alabama A&M. Elizabeth Jones passed away in 1927 in Dayton, Ohio. Sometime after her death (perhaps as late as 1930), Jones went to Omaha to live with Louise Kelly, whom he called his foster mother. It is unclear when this was and how much back and forth there was to Alabama and why. During this period he also worked as a golf caddy and a boxer. By the late 1920s, he was working as a drummer (though he also played piano and trumpet) throughout the Midwest. He also claimed to have been Tap Charleston champion of the United States for a year and a half during this period. He must have gone through stretches of feast and famine, because at times he would hobo with his drum kit on trains and at other times he would run bootleggers from Oklahoma City up to Minneapolis and back in his special-model Cadillac, of which only a few were made. The others belonged to Al Capone and to "Burt, the gangster that got killed in Memphis." He also worked as a farmer on a twenty-one-acre parcel he owned (or perhaps leased) outside of Omaha.

Meanwhile, as a musician, he slowly worked toward a revolution in drumming. When he was only twelve or thirteen he played drums for the prolific musical-comedy husband/

wife team Butterbeans and Susie.[3] (He remained close to them for many years.) Jones was working as a jazz musician, as opposed to a circus/carnival musician, by the late 1920s. He played with a wide variety of bands across the Midwest and first recorded with Lloyd Hunter's Serenaders in 1931. In 1934 he joined Count Basie in the famously raucous, good-time town of Kansas City. Under the Pendergast political machine, Kansas City became a haven for unparalleled nightlife, which included alcohol (during Prohibition) and gambling. This created ample work for musicians, and through the sort of laboratory created by the many venues and jam sessions, styles of playing across the Midwest and Southwest came together in a new style that had more swing than ever before. Other places, such as Oklahoma City, played a key role as well, but everything fell into place in Kansas City, most famously under the direction of Count Basie, with the crucial assistance of Jo Jones, Walter Page, and others.

Phil Schaap told me a tale that illustrates something special about the giant musical laboratory of 1930s Kansas City. Jerry Jerome (who played with Benny Goodman and later became a physician) and Skitch Henderson (the prominent conductor) both told Schaap—at a twenty-five-year remove from one another—the tale of a mythic-sounding venue that was the toast of the town. The front room was a dance hall, and this is where most respectable citizens congregated. The connected could get into the next room, an illicit gambling parlor. Beyond the gambling parlor was an even more special and secret room, an inner sanctum, a sort of musical holy of holies where only the truly hip could enter, that featured the early sparks of a jazz revolution: Count Basie on piano and Jo Jones on drums. Jones always said that the Basie odyssey began (and ended) with piano and drums.

Jones played with Basie's original 1934 band that broke up in Little Rock, Arkansas. He said many times that he was the last one by Basie's side when that first band broke up. He would play with Basie again in Bennie Moten's band, then again, after Moten's untimely death, with the regrouped Count Basie band that exploded out of Kansas City in 1936, conquering Chicago and, by Christmas Eve of that year, New York City. They then proceeded to swing America like crazy through the late thirties and early to mid forties with their Kansas City insouciance, changing music forever and becoming one of the most beloved bands in the history of music. The ins and outs of what happens next have been told many times, but never as colorfully as Jones does in this book.

Basie's band excelled artistically and commercially for the next decade and a half. The band was crowded with geniuses and innovators: Basie, Walter Page, Freddie Green, Lester Young, Buck Clayton—but Jones was key. According to Buck Clayton, "Jo had an *attitude* that got us all going in the Basie band. Every time he and Pres sat down, they wanted to swing."[4] Burt Korall has written that the Basie band "altered the conception of how jazz could and should be played. By exploring natural, flowing pulsation and marrying it to relaxation, the band offered a fresh approach to soloing and sectional and ensemble performances."[5] Nobody ever swung like them, and they made other bands sit up, take notice, and adjust accordingly. As Albert Murray told me, Basie even made Duke Ellington change gears and smooth out his swing.

Jo Jones played with Basie from 1936 to 1944. They traversed the country back and forth playing huge engagements and small one-nighters, meanwhile recording some of the most influential and memorable music in the history of jazz, such as "Cherokee," "Jumpin' at the Woodside," "One O'Clock Jump," "Panassie Stomp," "Doggin' Around" (a favorite of Albert Murray), "Five O'Clock Whistle" (a favorite of mine), "Topsy," "Swingin' the Blues," "Lester Leaps In,"

and so many more. It's amazing just to list those records and
hard to believe that such things were ever created. It's like
contemplating the pyramids or Stonehenge.

Aside from knocking out a policeman in Pittsburgh in
1937 and being briefly institutionalized in a hospital for the
criminally insane, all seems to have gone fairly smoothly
for Jo during the height of the swing era. He was a major
star, handsome, well dressed, and a standout in a band that
was in high demand in America and included enormous
personalities.

He spent late 1944 through early 1946 in the U.S. Army,
reaching the rank of Tec 5. He never served outside the
United States. He received the Good Conduct Medal and is
buried in Calverton National Cemetery on Long Island. Un-
like his close friend Lester Young, Jones seems to have had
a rather ho-hum military experience. Portions of his records,
like those of so many others who served, were damaged or
destroyed by a 1973 fire at the National Personnel Records
Center in St. Louis. Michael James once suggested to me,
or said that he had heard, that Jones had a crackup (as they
called it back then) in the army, and this is how he actually
met Dr. Karl Menninger, as opposed to meeting him at the
Kansas State Fair in 1930, as he claims in the book. There is
no extant evidence to support this.

When Jones was discharged from the army in February
1946, he immediately rejoined the Basie band in the studio
and recorded one of the most hard-swinging, no-nonsense
compositions they'd yet recorded, "The King." If anyone was
wondering whether or not Jo Jones still had it (and he was
wondering a little bit himself), he answered them with a re-
sounding *yes*. It is nice to imagine that the nearly palpable intensity that seems to exist on this record is due to Jones being
back in the fold and, more broadly, reflects America's victory
and postwar exuberance (which was soon to dissipate). "The

King" seems to me to be, and perhaps someone has said this before, a kind of mighty exclamation point on the swing era. Jones left Basie in 1948 and pursued a successful and varied career as a leader and sideman until his final performance in Providence, Rhode Island, in November 1984.[6]

As hard as it may be to believe, there was so much more to Jo Jones than his being a dynamic character or a legendary jazz musician. Buck Clayton writes in his autobiography that Jones "was very lively and always had something going on."[7] From his father he must have inherited a certain aptitude for numerical-spatial thinking as well as superb hand-eye coordination. Jo Jones and Mike James were strolling down Second Avenue one warm sunny afternoon. They encountered a man who was laying bricks. The man was a jazz enthusiast who recognized Jones and halted his bricklaying in order to chat with him about music. He was an amiable fellow, and the three men talked for some time. After a while the bricklayer made a comment to the effect that playing music was easier than the difficult task of laying bricks. Without comment, Jones proceeded to pick up the man's trowel and began to rapidly lay bricks perfectly and evenly, with the right amount of mortar and everything else appropriate to the task. Mike and the bricklayer were dumbfounded as Jones continued to lay brick after brick at a fast clip. When he finished, Jones said to the man: "I can do your job. But can you do mine?"

He was also a top checker player. In a 1991 *New York Times* article on the city's great checker players, checker master James Searles described what it was like to play Jo Jones: "'He beat me so bad,' Mr. Searles chuckled. 'He was a hell of a checker player.' He used to say, 'Boy, if I could play drums the way I play checkers!' But he made those drums talk."[8] As Haywood Henry recalled, Jones could "take his front line off the board and still beat us."[9] Jones was also a superb tennis player. As he remarks in the book, he has led the same life as many musicians, but they have not led the same life that he has.

There was another side to his personality, one that Phil Schaap comments on in his Afterword; it was a demanding side that eventually caused some people (perhaps including Basie) to become impatient with him. Jones could be exceptionally difficult with people at times. He used to be harsh in his critique of other musicians, and even if he was simply giving them a hard time, there were few who could calm him down. One such person, according to Michael James, was Duke Ellington's longtime drummer Sonny Greer (1895–1982). One night in the original Beefsteak Charlie's, a popular jazz musicians' hangout in 1960s Manhattan, Jones was haranguing some younger musician (as he often did) about what the younger man had not witnessed in the old days. Sonny Greer, with sympathy for the younger musician, said, "Oh, come on, Jo, I was getting drunk with the Prince of Wales when you were still picking cotton in Alabama." Jones took it well, coming from Mr. Sonny Greer who, along with Mr. Benny Carter, Mr. Wilson Driver, and a few others, Jones paid his ultimate personal compliment by calling them "Mister." At the same time, he was well known for cheering up and encouraging younger musicians by addressing them by the name "Young Talent."

While Jones was notoriously volatile and difficult, he was also fiercely loyal and kind to old friends. On the same day (according to Clayton) that he recorded the trippy, spacey, experimental album *Percussion and Bass* with Milt Hinton, Jones came across his old friend Buck Clayton in a sorry state in a jazz club in Paris. Clayton had just found out that he might never be able to play the trumpet again, and he got so drunk that he didn't know "where I was nor why I was there."[10] Jo Jones watched over him for the night and got him home.

This was part of the Basie band bond. As Jones told Dan Morgenstern, "I traveled for fourteen years with a bunch of *men,* and there was not one fight."[11] "The band," said Jones at another time, "operated on a strange spiritual and mental plane."[12] Let us return to that "raggedy band" (as Jones lovingly referred to them, perhaps evoking Robin Hood's Merry Men) and their musical heights.

As masterful artists, the Basie band members were highly conscious of, yet lighthearted toward, their massive achievements. The musicologist Mark Tucker has explained how the band spelled out its innovation:

> "Twelfth Street Rag" (1939) gives a summary of Basie's preferred techniques. After a deliberately old-fashioned introduction Basie states the theme with exaggerated squareness as Jo Jones adds "period" breaks on wood blocks. Then in the second chorus, Basie and his rhythm section give an updated, swing era response to ragtime. The evenly pulsing four of Page, Jones, and guitarist Freddie Green, together with Basie's [Fats] Waller–[James P.] Johnson treble figuration make the piece swing instead of stride.[13]

This sounds like it was a sort of educational recap of what they'd done three years earlier (and did over and over in the intervening years). Tucker writes of their 1936 version of "Oh, Lady Be Good" (recorded under the name Jones-Smith, Inc., for Jo and Carl "Tatti" Smith, due to record label politics), "Here, for the first time on record, is the classic Basie style. The left hand has virtually disappeared and the right-hand phrases have more space between them as Basie floats high above Walter Page's bass and Jo Jones's high-hat cymbal."[14] The new conception of the role of the high-hat, or as Jones often called it, the sock cymbal, constitutes one of his crucial innovations. As Jones notes on *The Drums,* "I was the only *bum* out here with a sock cymbal."

As Burt Korall described it, "When drummers discovered the possibilities for sticks on the high-hat the general nature of time-keeping radically changed.... Jones was primarily responsible for moving the time to the high-hat and suggesting what could be done on cymbals."[15] Most chroniclers of the history of jazz drumming have focused on this aspect of Jones's contribution, but according to Milt Hinton, there was another, related aspect of what made his playing special: "[Jones] played drums like he was a violinist. He could control his sound and actually had the ability to change his pitch for soloists. Years later when I ran jazz workshops, I tried to teach drummers what Jo did, but soon I realized it can't be taught."[16] Jones demonstrates on *The Drums* the way he'd change pitch to back different instruments. The composer and musicologist Gunther Schuller, in his book *The Swing Era,* has summed up Jones's musical achievement:

> The last member of the rhythm section to be freed for melodic duty was the percussion, the drum set. Here, too, an early leader in this development was Jo Jones, the drummer in the Basie rhythm section for many years. His early recordings with Basie in 1936 reveal that he had already transformed the percussion from its earlier, solely time-keeping and mostly vertical sounding role into a melodic-linear one, in which cymbals, with their ringing capacity and their ability to elongate sound, became a new voice in the horizontalization and linerarization of jazz, and with this last innovation swing was finally achievable.[17]

Perhaps a result (or cause) of this development was the fact that Jones was in the vanguard of drum tuning. The jazz critic Whitney Balliet stated this poetically when he wrote that Jones had a drum roll "as smooth as hot fudge being poured over marble" and that he "grants" a "sparkling force" to the musicians he backed.[18] His style has perhaps never been described better than by Gary Giddins:

In his music all is dignity and grace, a controlled eupho-
ria and a cosmopolitan elegance that nonetheless—here
comes the jazz paradox—stimulates a divine fever. Or as
Jo used to say, he could "swing you into bad health."

Giddins also notes that Jones "turned the highhat into a red
alert for dancers round the world." In describing a 1970s
Jones performance at the West End in upper Manhattan,
Giddins writes that "every set was a stream-of-consciousness
montage of music, humor, dancing, reminiscing, acerbic
asides."[19]

I hope that *Rifftide* conveys the flavor of what the verbal
dimension of one of those sets was like, while at the same
time also filling in a major slice of the historical record and
offering substantial reflections on life, music, show business,
and the personalities Jones encountered in sixty years on and
off stage. Giddins writes that in the audience at the West
End one night (indeed many nights) was Albert Murray, who
said of Jones (as quoted by Giddins), "They should put his
face on coins."[20]

Jo Jones and Albert Murray

Rifftide, in a sense, grew out of *Good Morning Blues: The
Autobiography of Count Basie,* as told to Albert Murray
(b. 1916). Murray began working with Count Basie on
what would become *Good Morning Blues* in 1976. In 1977,
Murray sat down with Jo Jones to collect background information for Basie's book. Over the next eight years, Murray recorded fourteen tapes of interviews with Jones. The
first tape appears to have been recorded on December 15,
1977, although not all the tapes have dates on them. The last
one was recorded in July 1985, shortly before Jones passed
away and in the year *Good Morning Blues* was finished. It is
quite possible, although not certain, that had *Good Morning*

Blues never come about, Murray and Jones still would have worked on some kind of a book together.

Jones and Murray first met, according to Murray, at Tuskegee Institute, around 1950, where Murray had attended college (1935–39). Murray was teaching there, following pre-war graduate study in pedagogical theory at Northwestern University, the University of Chicago, and the University of Michigan, after spending time in the Army Air Corps (1943–46), and after postwar study in literature at New York University (M.A., 1948). During World War II Murray attended (nonsegregated) Army Air Corps Officer Candidate School in Miami Beach (after Clark Gable, but with Ben Hogan) and later assisted in the training of the Tuskegee Airmen. (By August 1945 he was stationed in Denver, working on the logistical plans for an invasion of Japan.) In the fall of 1950, after several months studying in Paris at the Sorbonne via the G.I. Bill, Murray was recalled to service in the Air Force, and his teaching duties at Tuskegee shifted from the English Department to the ROTC program. He continued teaching in the ROTC program until he was transferred to the U.S. Air Force base in Morocco in 1955.

Murray was a lively and engaging conversationalist and through his social skills became involved with bringing various celebrities to the Tuskegee campus to either speak or perform. In this capacity he was involved with arranging for Duke Ellington, Ralph Ellison, Sugar Ray Robinson, and others to visit Tuskegee. Murray and his wife Mozelle lived with their daughter Michele in a house on the faculty circle. Sometimes celebrities would stay with them for a day or two when visiting the campus. Nat "King" Cole, for instance, stayed with them while visiting Tuskegee. But Murray was not the only one involved with bringing public figures to Tuskegee. Louis Armstrong visited around this time, and this is when Murray first met him. It is in this context that Murray first met Jones at Tuskegee.

Jones left Count Basie in 1948 after having been part of his band since 1936, with a 1944–46 hiatus for military service. Jones was in demand. He toured at various times with major stars such as Ella Fitzgerald and Teddy Wilson and played in major productions such as Jazz at the Philharmonic and George Wein's Newport Jazz Festival and Wein's European tours. The reason for his visit to Tuskegee when Murray met him is lost to history, although Murray did mention that "he *may* have been traveling with Sugar Ray Robinson."[21]

Jones and Murray shared Alabama backgrounds, knew some of the same people, and became friends. By 1955 they must have known each other fairly well. That year Ralph Ellison wrote to Murray of the following encounter he had with Jones in Manhattan:

> I went into a store on Madison Avenue the other day
> and saw a slightly built, balding mose[22] in there stepping
> around like he had springs in his legs . . . and using his
> voice in a precise, clipped way that sounded as though he
> had worked on its original down home sound with great
> attention for a long, long time—a true work of art. I dug
> this stud and was amazed. I was sitting across the store
> waiting to be served when he got up and came across to
> the desk to pay for his purchase and leave his address—
> when the salesman made the mistake of asking him if he
> wasn't the Joe (pardon me, Jo) Jones.
>   Well man, that definite article triggered him. . . .
> His voice opened up like a drill going through thin metal
> and before you could say Jackie Robinson he had recalled
> every time he had been in this store, the style of shoes he
> bought and why he bought them and was going into a
> tap dancing description of his drumming school, politics,
> poon-tang in Pogo Pogo and atomic fission. . . . I thought
> I'd better get him out of there to cool him off. . . . I finally
> managed to tell him that I knew you and he calmed

down. . . . What a character! I'm afraid that he's not only
a great drummer, he is—in the colored sense—also a
fool.[23]

It is funny that Ellison's claiming to know Murray is what
calmed Jones down. Of course, Ellison's fool, that is, the fool
"in the colored sense" is a master comedian, an ironic wizard
of signification. Murray replied to Ellison's riff on Jones as
entertaining personality with his own riff on Jones as master
musician and aesthetic theorist, perfectly capturing Jones's
philosophy of art's moral imperative, a practical force for
personal improvement and growth, or as Kenneth Burke, a
favorite theorist of Murray and Ellison would say, "equipment for living."[24] Murray wrote back:

Good to hear you riffing like that. But then you're bound
to be riffing if you're cutting dots for that goddammned
Jonathan Jones. . . . Remember what he told that fay[25]
drummer that time. This poor square cat was clunking
and plunking up there on 52nd and one night he looked
out and there's old Jo sitting there not even looking.
Whereupon this cat falls to and commences to fair-thee-
well all but cook supper on them skins as only a grayboy
feels he's got to do. Sweated himself into a double krupa
trying to make old Jo take notice, then at the end of the set
he came over ands asked if he dug him. "You're distorting me, man," old Jo lectured him right then and there,
his teeth set into that razor-edged footlights not-smile, his
eyes crowfooted, his nose narrow, his voice nasal. "This
way, man, this way. Lighten up, lighten up and loosen up.
Watch your elbows, man. Watch your shoulders. What
you mad about? It's music, man, music, music. From here
man, here, here, here. It's heart and soul pardner. Man,
you're distorting the hell of me." Man, that cat didn't use
nothing but brushes for the rest of the night.[26]

Murray's response to Ellison's riff, aside from its humor, is crucial and profound because it concretely illustrates the basis of Jones's aesthetics while also shedding light on where their aesthetics converge. Jones said to Dan Morgenstern in 1965:

> To become a good jazz musician, you must try to hear and see things that are beautiful. Be like a sponge; absorb experience and play it. Music is therapy for people, and the most stimulating music there is is jazz. It is also the most spiritual of all the musics—a delicate thing. You can't play it unless you have found yourself and it takes time to find ourselves.[27]

This is not some dreamy nonsense from someone with his head in the clouds.[28] This is coming from someone who saw it all, who is frank about the terrible racism he experienced yet irreverent toward its sources, someone who explains the large role that organized crime played in the booking of musicians in the 1930s but does not wring his hands about it. In this case as in another important instance in *Rifftide,* Jones sounds very much like André Malraux, a thinker that Murray (and Ellison) found most important. Malraux writes, toward the end of his monumental survey of visual art *The Voices of Silence:* "In times when man feels stranded and alone, [art] assures to its votaries that deep communion which would else have passed away with the passing of the gods. . . . All art is a revolt against man's fate."[29] Malraux would have been at home with Jones and vice versa. For Jones art is both practical and spiritual, both a great mystery interwoven with the process of becoming and equipment for living.

For Murray, who has written about art extensively, art derives from the playful reenactment of survival techniques. He outlined his outlook in a 1997 interview:

Ritual reenactment supervised by a priesthood becomes religion, which also generates its own specific internal ceremonies of devotion and propitiation, which I mention only in passing, along with magic, which is another kind of ceremonial reenactment. In addition to religion and magic, there is also the no less aboriginal matter of playful reenactment, which we refer to as recreation, and which indeed is literally the matter of re-creation, re-presentation, and re-producing. Thus the essential character or disposition of a nation as well as a tribe may be discerned from its games and toys. But the key point of this brief natural history is that it is from the playful re-enactment of primal ritual that art as such is most directly derived. The role of play in the creative process is that it permits the personal options from which individual expression, improvisation, stylization, and elegance emerge.[30]

Duke Ellington wrote that music "began with man, primitive man, trying to duplicate Nature's sounds—winds, birds, animals, water, the crescendo of fire—after which great systems of learning were set up, only to discover that music is limitless."[31] It has been well established that the fully orchestrated blues statement (better known as big band jazz) relies on railroad onomatopoeia as sonic inspiration and proceeds to *swing* those train sounds. Fine explanations of this complex creative endeavor can be found in Albert Murray's *Stomping the Blues* (1976) or Joel Dinerstein's deeply researched study *Swinging the Machine: Modernity, Technology, and African American Culture between the World Wars* (2003). As Jones says on his album *The Drums* (1973), it was crucial that drummers learned how to "play the train."

But there was another aspect—a visual aspect—to Jones's playing that Murray so deeply admired. Jones's physicality and unusual arm movements behind the drums have often been commented on. According to Murray, who noted this

many times in discussions with me, Jones was playfully re-
enacting the arm motions used in picking cotton. Furthermore, this visual vocabulary was not lost on African American
audiences, particularly in the South. Murray himself picked
cotton in the summer of 1935, before going to college, for the
dual purposes of raising some spending money and because
he saw picking cotton as "something heroic" and wanted to
have the experience that so many of his people had before
he entered the world of higher education. Murray admired
Jones's creativity in this regard because through it Jones showed,
in a way that confirmed and affirmed some of Murray's deep-
est held beliefs, that the memory of cotton picking was not
something fated to break someone down but rather just another thing to be swung—more raw material for the creation
of art—all to Murray's ultimate purpose of giving texture to
consciousness and, finally, to achieving happiness.

Murray retired from the Air Force in 1962 with the rank
of major and moved to New York to begin his writing career. He published newspaper and magazine pieces throughout the 1960s, and in 1970 he published his first book, *The
Omni-Americans: Some Alternatives to the Folklore of White
Supremacy* (his preferred subtitle to this book that had two
in its publication history). He received widespread and im-
mediate attention, with *The Omni-Americans* garnering the
cover of the *Washington Post Book World* and reviews in
Newsweek and the *New Yorker*. Before he shifted gears
into working on a book with Count Basie, he published a
memoir that became a finalist for the National Book Award
(*South to a Very Old Place,* 1971), a critical study of the hero
in literature vis-à-vis the blues tradition (*The Hero and the
Blues,* 1973), an inventive, jazz-structured novel of growing
up in and around Mobile (*Train Whistle Guitar,* 1974), and
a history and aesthetics of jazz (*Stomping the Blues,* 1976).
Stomping the Blues must have been one of the "two books"
by Murray that, Murray writes, Count Basie "looked at" before

choosing him as his collaborator for *Good Morning Blues*. *Stomping the Blues* was admired by Jones, who riffs at one point that it is one of his most prized possessions ("Awards and stuff, I don't keep this junk. Only your book: I keep that.").[32] *Stomping the Blues* also became a sort of foundational philosophical text for what was to become Jazz at Lincoln Center.

On the first tape (December 15, 1977), although the focus was on collecting information for Basie's book, Jones pitches an idea to Murray for a short book to be called "Rhythm Section," a group of biographical sketches that he conceived on the personal and musical history of Basie's All-American Rhythm Section (Basie, Jones, Walter Page, Freddie Green) and that Jones would essentially narrate to Murray. "Now, that's a nice little paperback for you," Jones added. Murray seems intrigued by the idea, but neither Murray nor Jones ever bring up the idea of "Rhythm Section" again.

On later tapes, as the topics drift far from Basie, it becomes clear that Murray and Jones have a different purpose in mind. Jones tells Murray several times that this material will compose a book that he wants Murray to write. Murray had this in mind, but perhaps not as forcefully as Jones did at that time. Murray had committed to Count Basie first, and *Good Morning Blues* was a major Random House title in January 1986, its publication greeted with a book party of epic proportions at the Palladium (black-tie, a thousand people) and the full effort of the Random House marketing/publicity machine. Yet while Murray was writing it, he found time to sit down with Jones and record his intriguing discourses, hoping it would lead to a book. During these same years Murray was also working on his own fiction and nonfiction, teaching creative writing at Emory (1977–1978), Barnard (on and off in the early 1980s), and Colgate (1982), and collaborating with (and writing and lecturing about) the artist Romare Bearden.

As *Good Morning Blues* neared completion, Murray wanted to turn to a book on Jones. *Good Morning Blues* was essentially finished when Jones and Murray sat down for what would be their final interview in July 1985 (having done no taped interviews since 1982). Jones died on September 3, 1985, four months before *Good Morning Blues* was published. After spending time promoting *Good Morning Blues,* Murray turned his time and attention to two other projects: his own fiction, poetry, and nonfiction (resulting in six books between 1986 and 2005) and working to help develop the organization that would in 1996 become Jazz at Lincoln Center.

During these busy years, Jones could not have been far from Murray's mind because he based a character, a drummer named Joe States, on him in his last two novels, *The Seven League Boots* (1995) and *The Magic Keys* (2005). In those novels, the first-person narrator, Scooter, is a bass player traveling with a big band led by the Bossman, a bandleader based mostly on Duke Ellington and partially on Count Basie. Joe States is the band's drummer. States is a Jo Jones–like figure, but interestingly, Murray never has States say anything that Jones actually says on tape verbatim. Joe States is Jo Jones reimagined by Murray. For example, Jones says of Duke Ellington that he "wrote life" and that Murray and Ellison have the ability to "write life." Here is Joe States in *The Magic Keys:*

But what we don't ever let any newcomer to this outfit
forget is that we don't just play music in this man's band,
we play life. L-I-F-E, as in flesh and blood. And me and
you and old Spodeody and the man make the difference
between metronome time and pulse. Like I told you.
Metronome time is mathematics, Schoolboy. Pulse is *soul.*
Talking about rhythm and tempo of life as *the folks* came
to know it and live it in the *downhome* U.S. of A.[33]

In *The Seven League Boots,* for instance, Murray has Joe States riff on Jones's statement that musicians "played the incident" that they may have witnessed or been involved with at a gig or in a venue, that is, gave musical expression to something dramatic that happened. Joe States says:

> Everybody's always carrying on about how hip and out front this band has always been; but man, this stuff we play is also historical. Everything this band plays is connected with some kind of story about something that is flesh and blood and history, he said. And then he said, Old Pro is going to see to it that everybody is cutting them dots, but that's just a convenience like a map. It's always that little story that counts with him and the bossman.[34]

So that there is no confusion, Jo Jones is also referred to in the novels in passing (as is Duke Ellington). Joe States makes Jones-like statements and talks something like Jones, but he is most certainly *not* Jones. I have a feeling this may be because the real Jones, as Murray knew, may have been too intense to capture.

JO JONES: HIS WORDS IN CONTEXTS

When Murray first told me about the tapes, he said that they reminded him of James Joyce's final masterwork, *Finnegans Wake,* a dreamlike book (supposedly the tale of a dreaming mind), full of digressions, written entirely in an English-like language of puns. When we were playing around with ideas for titles, Murray joked with calling the book "Finnegans Wake in Jive" or "The Jive Dimension of Finnegans Wake." This does not do justice to the complexity of *Finnegans Wake,* which is why the idea was quickly dropped. But the point that Murray was getting at was that Jones's jive and

Joyce's blarney are close cousins. Both are highly creative forms of discourse that fly under the radar of official culture, created by groups that were once, and in some cases are, far from the seats of power and official discourse. Often they pose challenges to official discourse and do not worship its pieties. They topple its false idols and belly-laugh or raise an eyebrow at its pretensions. Black Americans have linguistic games like "the dozens" and techniques like signifyin', rhetorical games that people engage in with each other in a bar or barbershop or barbeque. The Irish have similar linguistic game-jousts but call it "craic." At any rate, Jones's digressions reminded Murray (and me) of James Joyce. These mysterious Irish affinities may have also prompted Jones to record one of his greatest tunes as a leader, "Be Bop Irishman," with the Jo Jones Trio in 1959. Another tune Jones recorded during this era, "Spider Kelly's Blues" (composed by Ray Bryant), may refer to the Northern Irish boxer Billy "Spider" Kelly (1932–2010), who won the British featherweight title in 1954, or Billy's father, Jim "Spider" Kelly, a boxer who fought from 1912 to 1931.

Jones is part of two closely linked American traditions: the cavalier, devil-may-care, brash, confident, vernacular tradition and the exaggerated autobiographical tradition. The African folk and mythological traditions that morphed in the United States into the stories of Br'er Rabbit and the Signifyin' Monkey also informed both the literary and non-literary history of the United States. Under the umbrella of the vernacular falls the most "don't carified" blues lyrics (to borrow an expression from Murray's *Train Whistle Guitar*),[35] the playful boasts of Muhammad Ali, and some hip-hop braggadocio.

The second and closely related great American tradition that Jones finds himself in is the literary tradition of the exaggerated autobiography. This is not to say fabricated, just exaggerated, because informed by the vernacular tradition. Do you think he really pulled that many guns on that many people? I can authoritatively say *yes*, he did. He probably only told us about half the guns he pulled. Also, I hereby declare that a narrative cannot be a part of this grand tradition if it's exaggerated in the direction of the sappy or maudlin. That makes it something else, like the drippy opposite of a good old-fashioned frontier brag. What parts have been fabricated? Maybe none of it. Maybe much of it. Ain't for you to know. Why? 'Cause it's all true, that's why.

It means that the concern is less with what actually happened than with what the narrator is going to say happened, because he or she is ultimately something of a frontier bragster at heart. In this regard, Jones stands tall alongside such figures as Benjamin Franklin, Mark Twain, Zora Neale Hurston, and Ernest Hemingway.

There is yet one more tradition in which Jones finds himself, and that is the grand tradition of downplaying, underreporting, or underacknowledging one's level of education or sophistication. This is a tradition, often commented on by Ellison, that leads from Thomas Jefferson to William Faulkner and beyond. Jones read voraciously and owned a large library but did not seem to be invested in the idea of being an intellectual or a representation of one. He was an intellectual, and since he was an original in every other way, he was an original intellectual as well. The way he talks about the books he loves feels totally natural. Meanwhile, Jones is unabashedly proud of his deep knowledge of show business. And why shouldn't he be? At some level, most business is a form of show business. The phrase "show business" has perhaps developed pejorative connotations, but before the days of grants and teaching jobs and the arts institutions of late capitalism (or whatever), great artists like Armstrong, Ellington, Basie, and Ella Fitzgerald had to thrive in the world of show business.

Furthermore, I don't know if any artist on the level of Jones, save for perhaps Armstrong, has ever been quite so disarming and self-deprecating. Even when Jones is bragging, he can be disarming. He frequently referred to the trade he mastered as "ding-digga-ding," as in, "I was out there playing, you know, ding-digga-ding." I can think of few better descriptions that could be applied to Jones than this one from the poet and art critic John Ashbey, writing of his good friend the painter Fairfield Porter. Ashbery is, of course, taking the term "know-nothing," which often refers to an ignorant, nativist strain in American politics, and turning it on its head and retooling its meaning to celebrate a strategy common to several great American artists:

> Porter was, of course, only the latest in a series of brilliant know-nothings who at intervals have embodied the American genius, from Emerson and Thoreau to Whitman and Dickinson down to Wallace Stevens and Marianne Moore. Her title "In Distrust of Merits" could stand for them all. . . . [Porter's works] are idea, or consciousness, or light, or whatever. Ideas surround them, but do not and cannot extrude themselves into the being of the art.[36]

I'd like to add Jones to that club. He didn't wear his vast learning on his sleeve. He reveled in humor and let his intellect gently inform rather than overwhelm his music. The fact that he did not win the NEA Jazz Master award in one of the first three years of its existence (1982, 1983, 1984) and when he really could have used the money really throws the phrase "In Distrust of Merits" into relief. (He won it in 1985.) Jones certainly embodied the American genius in his time as much as those on Ashbery's list. Ashbery's theory about art and ideas connects back to Jones's statement to a young white drummer, quoted by Murray in that letter to Ellison: "What you mad about? It's music, man, music, music. From here, man, here, here, here. It's heart and soul, pardner."

Jones was a special figure—in jazz history, in American history, heck, in the history of the world. Loren Schoenberg, Benny Powell, Milt Hinton, Phil Schaap, Roy Haynes, Albert Murray, and others have all noted the same thing about him: his regal bearing. What Jones said about Duke Ellington we also have the honor to say about him: he's not dead—he's alive on the page and in his music. Long live the king!

Riptide

I Have Had a Varied Life

The things that I have, I'll give to you. This is my legacy with you, *Albert*.[1] This is my last hoo-rah. I will not give this wealth of information to nobody else because they don't know how to handle it. You know what I mean? Mr. Murray, it's hard for me to tell these people I'm not impressed. But what I'm in with you, I'll put you way ahead, I'll give you so much material, goddamit, you'll have to lock yourself up and be all fucked up.

You must print what I have. I have enough to tell the real story. I came through W. E. B. Du Bois. Not Erskine Hawkins, not those peoples. They never met nobody.

A lot of people ain't gonna fit with me and you. Now the only person that I know that can fit with you and I is Invisible Man,[2] *because Langston Hughes is not here.* I don't know who to talk to!

Take me forty-something years to earn my keep. I'm fifty-six years in show business. I have earned my keep. There won't be but two people in the United States can tell you.

Now ask the president of France. I got my picture with the president of France. You know what I'm saying? But I'm in something heavy. Like when I go down with Grace Kelly; she's got Josephine Baker's thirteen children! I'm with the policeman that held the umbrella overhead when they're dispossessing her.[3] See, I'm kinda odd out here.

I sleep with my door unlocked, me and my Bible. My friend comes in, she locks the door. I've never locked my door in fifty-six years. Everybody understands how I play: I play free. I'm not afraid of a living person. I fear *God:* I got four hundred religions and five hundred cults. There are two people that give me strength: Billie Holiday and Lester Young.

In 1923 I met Lord Beaverbrook. In '24 I had to do a thing with another act that's with Rudolph Valentino: three weeks. Then I met Harry Houdini! Then Jack Dempsey! I used to ride the street car on credit and be up there talking to the motorman. Shit, I can't sit back there with everybody else: I ain't got no money!

I came out with the second coming of the covered wagons in the carnival shows and circuses. I've been in the alleys and byways.[4] Most people have never been in the forty-eight states. Forty-eight states: I know the district attorneys—not only that, I'm in Interpol! And I always keep my fare home.

A book on Jo Jones won't sell. You don't wanna get into my personal life. I've never done anything sensational. A book on Jo Jones won't sell—it's too dry. It's no knock-down, drag-out affair. If you *really* want to do a book on Jo Jones— you couldn't sell it anyway. I'll close up the U.N.! I'd stop all wars if you get into *my* life.[5] I'll pull all the dirt from under the rug! I'ma give you what you *supposed* to write about *me. My book.* You gonna do it. Wait 'til you get to *that shit*! 'Cause all these things, these territories, these eleven states—I cover the whole thing! I'll put you way ahead.

Listen man, I've had a hell of a time. See now, I cover a whole lot of shit. I cover the Selmas, the Mobiles; I cover the Chattanoogas; I cover the Tri-cities; I cover the Louivilles; I cover Paducahs; I cover Texas, Brownsville; I cover—I've been out here, I've been in many things. I have had a *varied* life.

Can't Nobody Tell Me One Inch about Show Business

They spend billions of dollars to kill people. We are trying to help people. We are trying to *entertain* people. How someone gonna tell me he don't sing as good as she don't dance as good as he don't play good as—I'm not interested in that. We know who's *the best*. We got a commodity that you can't *buy*.

Don't put nobody in front of me, from *Bob Hope* up: they can't tell me one inch about show business. I covered the whole thing, the Bob Hopes, the theater. I covered the whole sphere. I knew the dancers. I knew the musicians. I know how everybody feels. I've been those things and I was always a nut. I was the Tap Charleston champion of the United States for a year and a half.

I've never been a sad musician. There are things I don't talk to the layman. There are certain things I don't talk to the sad man, 'cause he don't know what's happening. These front-runners: I'm through with them for the last three years. What's wrong with you jokers? Don't you know how to handle your business? You got an agent? You got a manager?

You got an accountant? You gonna do all that *and* play *and* pay them? Let the agent argue. Say: talk to my agent, I don't know nothing about that. You ain't got nothing to do but come to work. You need all that energy to get in front of that public.

Out of the Fat, into the Fire

We in Kansas City.[1] Here's a guy come up to me and says, "HEY, YOU." You talking to me? "Yeah. You going to St. Louis to play in my club." I wondered why them little boys didn't say nothing to this man when this man told me I was gonna leave and go to St. Louis, 250 miles away. I'm lookin' at these little boys, I say, shoot, I know damn well they got *me* protected. I'm the pet! But they didn't say nothing to this man. He just left from Sing Sing—the death row! It was *Jim Scarpelli* from the Plantation in St. Louis.[2] He looked like Thomas Gomez.[3] I said, "You talkin' to me? Man, you outta your cotton pickin' mind."

I get to St. Louis, I'm over with Jimmy Swanson, and the club is next door. I was playing checkers. I was hanging out with Fate Marable. They sent a waiter for me to catch the show. I'm playing checkers, man. I was taking Sid Catlett's place 'cause he was playing with Fletcher Henderson. They sent another one *[waiter]* over there. I said, "I'm playing checkers!" Man, look, I ain't going nowhere. Finally I went over, I said, "What do y'all want?" "We want you to catch a show." I know what the show is doing, you ain't got nothing like in Kansas City.

In St. Louis I got into a ruckus over there with one of the boys. He had his two pistols. He was tellin' me about the cigarette girl. I said I'm not bothering her. He said, "Oh, you're tough." I said, "No, sir." I said, "Why don't you take one of your pistols and give it to me, just lay it here, and let's go for a set." I said, "It's *your* pistol, I don't know anything about you." "Oh, you can shoot?" "Yeah!" That's when I go downstairs and start shooting corks out of bottles—with their pistols! CLACK, CLACK, CLACK. CLACK, CLACK, CLACK. Frank B. Hart taught me how to shoot! I said, "I don't bother none of your chicks, they bother me." He was bad; he was a triggerman, you know. I had to sneak out of St. Louis.

I played on a Sunday in East St. Louis. Chick Webb was there. I didn't get a chance to enjoy Chick Webb. While everybody was enjoying Chick Webb, I said, "Take me to the bus station." I came back to Kansas City. When I walked into the Booker T. Hotel, Stidget Wilson was the manager. He gave me a dollar. I got a taxi and went down to the Reno. This was the summer of 1936.

When I came back from St. Louis I was on Eighteenth Street. I was standing with Basie, Joe Keyes, and Lips. They said, "Don't go down there, 'cause Charlie Ryan's gon' *kill you!*" I said, "Come on, Basie!" We walked in the place and there's Charlie Ryan standing there. He said, "You got..."

I said, "Don't say it! Give me a half a pint of gin, and Basie's gonna drink it and give me five dollars, and I'll go back to St. Louis and get my drums." A last wish? Know what I mean? Know what I mean? You'd give a man his last wish, right? Ryan was the man they sent to prison for life for the great big mail robbery. He did three months on Long Island and came back. So I said, "Wait a minute, come on Charlie, since you're gonna kill me, give me my last wish. Give me that half pint of gin. We sat in that club, in that white club, and Basie sat in there drinking. I stopped Charlie cold. Last wish! Basie drank up the gin, a man ate a hearty meal. Charlie Ryan, when he found out about my background, he left me alone.

I had been caught up in a range war before. That's how I got into Kansas City, leaving Frank Hart. This is a story you've got to hear, and every criminal will bear me out, man. They put guns in his ribs and said, "Where's that boy?" That's how I left Omaha to join Tommy Douglass. I ran out of the fat into the fire. Everywhere I went I've always been 'round some people. See? I gone through this thing in Omaha 'cause the man had fired the colored band and told me I was gonna play with the white band. I said, "No, I ain't. I'm going with him." They said, "No, you ain't." I'm there by myself. His little henchman say, "Lemme hit him, boss." I said, "Why don't you hit me, Frank? I weigh a hundred and thirty-five and so do you—you do it. They had these big guys, big as Walter Page, but they knew if they fooled with me, the boys down on Thirteenth Street would come up and wreck the joint. Cloverleaf Club, I'll never forget it. But when they found out I was going to work for Frank Yousum, that was different. He was a legitimate man, but Frank Hart was on the other way. He's the man taught me how to shoot! Oh, m'gosh. I'm sittin' in the window playing at another club and there is Frank Hart coming in, going to the bar, looking at me. I'm thinking, I'm sitting up here in this window, and they'll throw anything—a garbage pail—in here! I split and go to Kansas City, of all places, and run into a hornet's nest again. Leaving Omaha, I thought I was free, but I ran from one gangster into another.

We Understand They Took the Big Bands Away

I just got through slapping somebody in France, telling me bout Norman Granz. He said, "Norman Granz should be ashamed, he ain't doing nothing but killing Ella Fitzgerald." I said he's doing what? Do you know Ella Fitzgerald? I've been snoring in her face since 1937. First she married a cigarette, then she married Ray Brown. Every time she gets ready to marry somebody, I step in. Norman's come to me ten times, said, "Tell her!" I said tell Ray Brown. Ray says you knew her before me, you tell her. She *will not,* as of today, sit down. She just got to be out, she just got to be out here. Let's go! She's Ringling Brothers, she's carrying a load, you know.

Everybody says, man, we going to Las Vegas, we going, we going. I say no shit! See, Freddie Green has slept in my mother's home in Omaha. Danny Barker was there for three days. For two weeks, Teddy Wilson. See, everything that slept in my mother's backyard in Omaha opened up Las Vegas when it was a fuckin' whistle stop. You'd look out there and you'd see two lights.

Bugsy Siegel was married to Virginia Hill. OK? She died in Switzerland. She was in Omaha.[4] I was playing footsies with her in the sandbox! I'm glad I didn't go to bed with her. That's why I can do what I want to do. You never go to bed with the boss's daughter. That's why I have a lifetime contract. I can play anywhere. I saw Dorothy Donegan five or six years ago, and she said, "*That man* wouldn't touch me!" You don't go to bed with the boss's daughter.

Now the boy that just left Las Vegas to go to Atlantic City: he had a cookhouse at Caesar's Palace, so he went to Las Vegas, he was the head of Caesar's Palace. Where is he now? He's in Atlantic City. When he was at Lake Tahoe, at Harrah's, he said if you come out here and do sixteen weeks, I'll give you that Model T Ford you want. I said I'll do four weeks. I don't gamble no more. Said, why 'on't you come out here? I said shit, fuck that place! I don't want to stay in New York four weeks!

The biggest mistake our guys make when they want to join a group: they don't get the records. Like a boy I was talking to. He's gonna get a job playing with Ella Fitzgerald. He don't know nothing about Ella Fitzgerald, but seen her. Now he's gonna sit there with Tommy Flanagan? Ain't no big band, she's using a trio! He don't know nothin' 'bout that shit! What you do: you go get you some Ella Fitzgerald records and your tape recorder, and when you're not doing nothing, when you're on the road, play two hours' worth of Ella Fitzgerald. Don't play no other shit, so when you get there, you will think Ella Fitzgerald.

If I know I'm recording with Teddy Wilson tomorrow, I'll play two hours of Teddy Wilson. Before I leave the house I'm a-play one hour. I don't wanna hear no music but Teddy Wilson. If I'm playing with Hank Jones, that's all I want to hear. Now I got Roy Eldridge, I ain't playing nothing but Roy Eldridge records. I don't wanna hear Sweets, I don't wanna hear Louis Armstrong, I don't wanna hear Dizzy "Guwespie,"[5] or nobody. *That's my training.* If I gotta play for Carrie Smith, I got Carrie Smith's record. These are things that's hard for me to pass on to guys 'cause there's so much distractions out here. And they get carried away, so what can you do about that? They get carried away with their write-ups, instead of taking it in stride and saying thank-you and keep going.

Jimmie Lunceford had two things going for him. The style of Lunceford's band. Willie Smith. Who made the beat? *Jimmy Crawford.* The style—boom. Willie. Willie can't go but two ways: he's got to go through Johnny Hodges or Benny Carter. Sy is there, but he don't learn nothing till Eddie Durham get there. He does not know how to voice arrangements like Eddie Durham. He will not arrange one-twentieth like Eddie Durham can arrange. He wanted to stay down in the office, for twenty dollars more, and arrange and rehearse the band. Lunceford said this is it. Tommy Dorsey said I'll take it.[6]

We understand that they took the dance floor away. We understand they took the big bands away. We understand they took everything away. Where's a kid going to serve his apprenticeship? We are trying to establish our farm system. You don't take a kid who's a good shortstop in Central Park just because he made a good play, and the Yankees are playing the World Series, you say, come on, you gonna play shortstop! What's he gonna do there? Those boys, when they come up from the minors, they gonna sit on the bench.

BLACK SHOW BUSINESS

I say to this guy, hey, you from Canada, you don't know about these people that I speak of. You don't know nothing about *black show business*. Every now and then somebody will tell you about Bert Williams, but if Bert Williams walked through this door they wouldn't know what he looked like. I said I know you wouldn't know what Garbage Rogers looked like, as sharp as he was![7] Some of these guys had to work in blackface: they was too light.

I went with Joe Louis and E. Simms Campbell up to St. Nicholas Avenue. There was a joker had a little joint there. He was from Canada. He had a girl in there, she looked like something something. She was a comedian. Man, she was *fast!* I used to take all the tennis players in there. We used to get pancakes there.

I know these comedians. The man say we can get Albert Murray for $200, another guy says I'll do it for $150. They say we got this joker for $150, the next guy says I'll do it for $125. Later on in life, when Slappy was with Tweedlee Dee,[8] Joe Glaser had to make out a contract. He was getting $350 a week on the same bill. And he had the man fix the contract out where it read $1,500. He's walkin' around tellin' the boys, "Hey, I'm make money, I'm making $1,500, man, let's have a drink." He's making $350. It's all publicity. They can do $3,500 and he ain't got but four hundred people there. It looks good.

We in this business, we go through a thing, and personally I've been very fortunate. Nobody's been more fortunate than me, living today. There's not one person who can walk in and sit down in this place and discuss show business with me, from A to Z. I was in the carnival shows and circuses, then I was a singer, a dancer, a dramatic artist, then I went through the trumpet, the saxophone, the piano, and now I'm the drums. And who knows why I play? I don't. I just have to play to keep alive, that's all.

Long Coats and Short Coats

A Negro band would be over here playing at the country club—but then they'd also have a white band. After them people get through going through them qua-drooles and stuff, they'd get over there and pick up where that *hot stuff* is,[9] you know what I mean? It was a long time before the long coats found out that the Negroes could read music. Because they didn't see no music! The long coat, he's got to read his stuff. The short coat would listen to it, and he would improvise. The long coat couldn't understand: you play the same thing but you don't see no notes. He didn't understand.

Long coat: that's whitey. Short coat: that's black. That's how I can talk about 'em faster.

OK. You got ten long coats. Only three in there know anything about rhythm. The seven had got to bring them down. You got ten short coats over here. Seven of these cats has got rhythm, they can pull these three up! You got ten black musicians but three of 'em ain't got no feeling. But if you keep hanging around there, with them seven, it's got to go. If you got ten whites, those three can't buck the system.

The first time that I catch a so-called white musician playing the blues, this is gonna be a happy world, because it's music and sports. I say, with all the technical and scientific know-how, I never get so sick and tired of little boys running round saying "let's play the blues." He doesn't even know how to pronounce blues. And he'll play C, E, and G but he wouldn't hit B flat, he'd hit B natural. With all his know-how! You know why that is? You might think it's a lie. Years ago the white folks would laugh first, and now you niggers laugh after that. That's where the laughing bell came in.[10] You didn't get to laugh until after the white folks got to laugh. You're up in that balcony, up in that peanut gallery.

WHERE'S THE SETTLEMENT? 'CROSS THE TRACKS!

The way we had to live? *The way we had to live?* Duke Ellington, he didn't have no better room. Basie didn't have no better room than us. He better be in that cold across the tracks, unless he knew some doctor or lawyer or somethin'. He stayed in them raggedy places where we stayed. He couldn't take off like no Benny Goodman, or hell, he *better* be 'cross the tracks. But at least the boys had they places to stay. Talkin' 'bout reading? You better know how to read! This is the white! Where's the settlement? 'Cross the tracks!

What about these kids that never had the system? Butch Miles? Where was he playing? A corner bar somewhere? Before a six-piece band? Man. He never played no shows. He never had no sixteen girls on his lap. He never played no thirty shows a week, four, five weeks at a stretch. He don't know what it is to sit on a bus to wait for someone to bring you a sandwich out. He can go anywhere. Four, five, in the morning: *he's white,* he can get something to eat. He don't have to stay with the band. He can get the itinerary and say goodnight fellas, and he's gone, back across the tracks. See what I mean? But he's trying, he's trying.

Some of the guys, well, they never did much traveling anyway. And then when they did travel, they didn't know what they saw. Man, we played one-nighters. Where did you go? We went down south. Where down south, where? Well, what did you see? Whom did you know? What did you do? Oh yeah, man, I remember this and so and so forth and so and so and so. I see. I say, I see, you know what I mean.

Jokers! You went to Atlanta? Yeah. You ever eat at Ma Sutton's? "Who?" I say never mind, you were never in Atlanta. You know some of the jokers. How long you in New York? Aw, so and so. You ever go to Ma Baker's on 126th Street? No, never went there. Oh you went to *Miss Frazier's*? Yeah, but you didn't go to Miss Frazier's when she was *down* the street, when you went on this side and played the numbers and went on this side to put your order in for the food. You know. Then she moved up, 'cross the street to the Theresa and became *elegant.* The food was nasty! You didn't want the food, it got too high-class. You know what I mean? Ahhh, shoot. But it's music and sports. It's always been.

The Harlem Globetrotters stayed in my place when they were making 35, 50 cents a night. That's why you cannot get one Globetrotter to call me Jo. They call me Mr. Jones.[11]

A WAY OF LIFE BEFORE WORLD WAR II

The Sunset Royals and these people, when they come up, that was all right, but we were in our thing. From '33 up to that time I been hanging out with the Grant Moores and the Eli Rices and Bennie Moten and then Count Basie by that time. We saw the Sunset Royals in passing. In all those bands you can't find nothing in there that is still playing now. It was a way of life before World War II. They just got in on it. They didn't know anything about economics, they didn't know anything about the social structure—it was just ha-ha, goody-goody-goody, and have a good time. They didn't think in terms of far ahead.

"Illi-noise" Jacquet, Cleanhead Vinson, and Arnett Cobb sat me down this year and said, are we doing right? They said you the only one used to come and sit with us, and you didn't let us drink Coca-Cola, made us drink lemonade, and run us home.[12] Cleanhead says I haven't been drinking in two years, and so forth and so on, my daughter's doing so and so, I'm doing this with her. Arnett said don't look at *me,* you changed my daughter's diaper. Jacquet just left here the other day, says you changed my daughter's diapers, boy, you know, she's gonna be a lawyer, she's down in Georgetown. He was telling Madame Therese[13] that they should make a movie 'bout his life, 'cause I've seen what he's gone through with his family. I said Jacquet, get outta here, she ain't supposed to know that. All the kids, they know me from the year one. If this is my forty-fourth year of changing diapers, where have I been?

See, these people don't know Teddy Wilson's *mother.* I knew Teddy at sixteen when he went to Talladega. Hold that! I don't know Teddy, I know his mammy and pappy. I don't know Max Roach. Max Roach was fourteen, Miles Davis was twelve. I know they mammy and pappy! I don't know Ray Bryant and them: I stood with the umbrella to bury his father. I don't take no shit from these people.

All these people, I know them here. I start with mother, father, sister, brother, aunts, and uncles—see, I can give them the address of where they were born. Now there were peoples that were with the Sunset Royals and what's his name, had that little band out of Flor-der. It's like a horse race, and you say, *there were many others.* Everybody knows who won the race if they've been playing horses twenty years. What was the fifth horse. Huh? But they remember the winner! Everybody was lookin' at that fight last night. They didn't see nobody but Muhammad Ali.

I said to Leonard Feather, the trouble with our business now is there's too many guys, they go home and listen to their records and read the write-ups. But I found out something different. They are *now* playing the write-ups and reading the records! You can see through the record. I found out that more nonmusicians have bought one of my records, and more musicians have bought it than drummers. The record sales. I said to the people at the store, I want you to ask people, when you sell this record, what's your profession? You know: doctor, lawyer, or Indian chief? Are you a drummer? Are you a saxophone player? It's an education record. They checked me out, gave me a balance sheet, and when I got the balance sheet, without IBM, more nonmusicians bought, next musicians, and the lowest ones that bought this record was drummers. Only one drummer bought this record twice: Louis Bellson. He keeps one at home and he travels with one, because I told him I made two mistakes on it. You know they've been looking for them two mistakes? I said, look fellas, it took me twenty years. I'll give you ten years to find them. I said I know I worked haaaard to make these two mistakes! They curious. You see in the first place, they didn't go to Bayview, to Mobile, to Selma, to Talladega, Chattanooga, Paducah, Lexington, Louisville. They don't know what Kansas City looks like!

A Different Kind of Living in That Southwest

The Yellow Front in Kansas City: Mary Lou Williams, Pete Johnson, Basie, everybody would be there. They'd come there after that club closed. There we were! And I'm sitting up there hoo-pawing on the piano, you know, trying to do stride, you know, Harlem Basie or some shit, Fats Waller or some shit. See, I wasn't thinkin' 'bout no drums, I wasn't thinkin' 'bout that, I had my vibraphones, you know. I didn't think I'd ever play drums—not for a vocation—'cause that's the reason I play the way I play. I don't play like nobody: I wasn't inspired. But I could absorb and knew the history and backgrounds of all these people, you know. Naturally, I was partial to comin' out of the Blue Devils. I was hanging out with Harry Smith, the Booker Pittmans. These guys were telling stories. And I could remember these stories. Shit, I wasn't good enough to work with Basie's band. What the hell would I be doing up there? That was a *band*. See, Basie had two bands that never came to New York and that's the end of that. That band was in Little Rock and there never will be a band like that. He could never assemble a band like that. We almost had it once, when I came out of the army. But it will never have that rapport, it will never have that intensity. Just the way it was supposed to be.

The drummer that went with the Norman Thomas Quintet was Rastus Crump. And he was a very sensational drummer. Naturally I used to do tricks and things with Kid Lips and things like that.[14] Every year they'd meet in either Detroit or Chicago. The contest would be in one town or the other. But I had to have a trick. I was in the middle of the women. I always had a trick. And I made one mistake with Kid Lips: He told me if I showed him my trick, he had a trick he'd show me. I showed him, but he didn't show me nothing! I showed him mine, but every time he was busy!

Here is what happened. Basie did exactly what Fats Waller did: all the guys that come under James P. Johnson, you know what I mean, and Willie "The Lion" Smith, they stayed playing that Harlem way, they didn't do the traveling, like Fats and Basie. Fats left and Fats was in the *byways* and *gone*. These other guys were *society*. Something happened when Basie got with the Blue Devils, there's something the way those guys played out there—different than they play out here—he's got to encroach on ya, that's how you've got all those records they made, like the "Shark" and "Layfayette" and all that in 1932. And he's gone! But you see, the guys in New York, they never played that way. They couldn't dig in like that.

And when you hear Fats Waller—all due respect to James P. or any of them—they did not have that because

Fats Waller—see, it's like on my record—you play according to the way you live. Harlem Stride, that was nice, that was pretty, but they didn't have that *thing*. Them boys was all right, they talkin' about the rent parties, but they never did the kind of living that Basie and Fats Waller got a chance to do—and Basie did a whole lot of living!—out there in that Southwest, from Texas, Oklahoma, Kansas, down in there, to Missouri. Hey, man! That's a different kind of living! The guys in Chicago never played like they played in Kansas City. The guys in the East? Forget it! They never had that. The Southwestern musicians, they had something. Every last one of them. They had a sound. And every trumpet player from that area. They had something.

As of today, you can go and hear 'em play today, tonight, put a musician on a plane and send 'em to Kansas City. Same group: they play different. Don't ask me what makes you play differently, I don't know. It's the spirit, it's something in there, I don't know what it is. And after they leave they can't play like that. Why did we play good in Kansas City and you don't play as good in Denver or Waco or Florida? Kansas City is the hearbeat. There's something about Kansas City spiritually. If you played like chicken shit last night, if you get in Kansas City you'll play your ass off, and you don't know *why*.

Puerto Rico

I'm glad I went broke in 1960. I had $85,000, and I thought I was on a ten-year plan. OK. When I went to San Juan, they will tell you today that I'm the one that's the cause of the musicians making money there. Nobody has ever been in that little place to raise the salary. You can talk to the president of that local, the secretary, and the treasurer. They swears by Jonathan David Samuel Jones. There is nobody been down there, from Sammy Davis to I don't care who go there—when I hit that island I did things that nobody ever did. Know what a man showed me in a vault? Four hundred million cash dollars. Sheeeit. I started something in San Juan, from 1960 up to now, nobody has ever done what I did to open up a vaccum. I've opened up joints, I've never closed one. Ain't no way in the world. Oscar Peterson? Couldn't get in there, has to go through me. The only way they can pay me back is to go and do a good job.

FRANCE

I leave on the third.[15] I arrive in Paris on the fourth. I catch a plane to Lyon. Somebody come up the street about sixty miles to pick me up and bring me down to Orange. I'll go in, I'll check in that night, that evening, say hello to people, go to the lavatory upstairs, check my blood out, and one of my other doctors will meet me up there. I'll stay overnight, get up the next morning, *promenade.* Now, what I'm supposed to do for a select group of people: they got this big yard, swimming pool, honeysuckle vines, and what have you. They got a little home over there already made for me. I'm gonna play just for a dog and a cat! With my wire brushes. After that, what happens? I'm due in Nice on the eighth of Ju-ly. On the eighth I draw Mary Lou Williams, Eddie "Lockjaw" Davis, and something, you know. On the ninth, I rest. On the tenth I got Gerald Williams and Milt Hinton. Good! On the eleventh, I got Hank Jones and somebody and also on the eleventh I got Ray Bryant and Milt. But! On the twelfth! I have to go over to stage two at a festival. That's the best stage. Stage one, two, and three: two is the best place. I'll have to be the guest of Mr. Buddy Rich. I'll play the hot ones, he'll play the sweet ones. Now, the thirteenth: I rest. On the fourteenth I'll have Jaws and somebody. Then on the fifteenth they want me to play for Helen Humes. I said, look, I didn't play for Ella Fitzgerald, why don't you let me play for Carrie Smith? But hey, look, I ain't gonna do nothing but play for it anyhow. Don't make no difference. But then I got a crazy idea. I always do something crazy. All the drummers. All these drummers and I wasn't going. They got all these drummers over there. Now I'm gonna have a luau with the damn drummers. I'm gonna have just my sock cymbal. On a lazy afternoon. All right fellas, you're working for me now! Look out! One, two, three! You know I'm a-do something wrong. I always do something wrong. But it's constructive. It's in good taste.

First program I did with children on television was on French television. I did the program, and then I had to do another one. I did it in Bordeaux. The director came down from Paris and said, "Jo, I can only give you a half an hour." I said good. I did an hour and a half. On TV! Language barrier? Now I got to do France, Spain, Italy, and Germany. On TV!—with kids from six to eleven. No language barrier. That's paid for by the state.[16] State! Not State Department: coal, iron, and steel you know, and oil. No. Nuh uh.

The Count Basie Institution

The Count Basie Orchestra was an *institution*.[1] It was like Notre Dame, it was like Vassar, it was like Oxford. It was like Eton![2] We had a guy who was a tailor, used to hang out with us. He said, thirty years after the fact, in front of his wife: "You hung out with the Basie band, you knew two things were gonna happen: you drank some booze and went to bed with some women! Hanging out with Duke Ellington was *nice,* it was *culture,* you know, I could get that at Carnegie Hall, but there's never been a band like that Basie band."

You're talking about CIA, FBI, or whatever: you were *screened* before you joined those kinds of bands. And see, once you got in there, that was you. I'll tell you how tight it was. See, if you took a man's place and he owed twenty dollars, you owed twenty. You owed his debt. You sittin' in his chair! "I did not . . ." Naw, you owed it! You got in the seat: you owed it. If your wife needed an operation or you needed a half a ton of coal, they'd give you the money, and nobody ain't said when you'd pay it back. Pay a dollar here, fifty

cents here. See, the environment you keep. Basie got into that
environment.

If you hang out with a group you can't go no other way,
you're gonna play in that vein. It's just a certain way that
they played, a certain way that the saxophone, that the trumpet and trombone played. You notice the Basie band, the
reason the band was flexible: everybody was a soloist. In the
other bands you had to write solo parts to get 'em to play
solo. They couldn't just stand up to play with a rhythm section. Right today, you don't know no band could do what
Basie's band did. You got to be *inspired.* And the spirit was
so strong there, you interchanged feelings, you interchanged
ideas. If you just sittin' around with the jokers playing the
notes and playing the notes, it didn't come out.

Basie got a chance to enhance his natural ability. Look
what kind of experience he had! Most of all your good piano
players, they did not play in no bands. Where they gonna?
You weren't gonna make no money in no bands: they'd play
in *whorehouses.* You got a chance to be like a sponge, you
absorbed the life that you saw. *You played the incident.* And
the guys used to make up tunes and put different titles on
them and make different licks, different riffs, you know. It
meant something. Every time they played something, it meant
something.

Every three or four weeks, they'd have the section. You
gotta work on him 'til he gets it. And then somebody else'll
take it. He could be a saxophone player, and if a trumpet
player liked that riff, if he could get to it, he's gonna play it.
See? If it's a thing one of them trumpet players play, you says
we got his ol' butt, you a saxophone player and you lookin'
right at that trumpet player and play his lick!

I joined Basie in 1934. I knew Basie before, I'd seen him
before, but I'd never thought I'd ever be associated with
any of these people—it was far from my thoughts. The first
time I run into Basie and Bus Moten they came over where

I was playing in south Omaha. They just come back from New York. Him and Bus got on the floor and they danced to "Sweet Sue." And me and Chuck lookin' at 'em said, *ain't that a bitch?* We got up and showed them how to dance!

Where the fuck they come from? These big-timers. They couldn't dance! Me and Chuck, we could dance! But I didn't think I was gonna meet these assholes no more. I begin to get around and ask different ones, and when I finally *did* begin to hang out, not thinking I'm a-play with these guys, but I got good answers to the questions I asked. Eddie Durham and these guys to this day have to ask me what *they* did. They'll say, was that right? I'll say no, that was another place. Goddamn!

When I got into Kansas City, I just knew those guys were making an awful lot of money. I had just left Omaha, Nebraska, man. I was making $22.50, see, working from nine to one. I didn't know them guys. Andy Kirk had the best job, he was only making $17.50. Basie was making $14 a week! I never thought I'd play with these guys. I'm still out there jitterbuggin', looking for autographs.

They had a bass player and a saxophone player who just tabbed up! That's a funny thing! To me, I'm starry-eyed, you know, I didn't know these jokers. Man, I thought these jokers got to be makin' $65, $70 a week! I'd just left Omaha, man, a little joint, joint about as big as the West End. They had horse players in there and I was making $22.50 a week and could walk to *woik*. Jeez! Room and board was $5 a week.

Shit, I was *nigger rich!*

You see, I was always hanging around from, say, 1930. If I went down to Oklahoma City, I was at a show. I could get a lot of information. I'd get the history about the different guys. I said I have to have a memory. The musical part: I knew the backgrounds of all the guys up to now. I knew them from year one. When I got to certain localities, where the guys were from, I made it a point to meet their mothers and fathers and brothers and sisters and aunts and uncles and meet the schoolteacher and who they played "I Spy" with. And I had something to say.

How Would You Like to Join Basie's Band?

Walter Page said, "How would you like to join Basie's band?" I said, *what?* I said, shoot, you know.

What brought it on was this: I was doing a one-nighter with Basie's band in Topeka, Kansas, and I was doing all right until they played "After You've Gone." Lester Young played the first chorus, and he was sittin' down, and when he stood up and took that second chorus, shit, I wanted to jump out the two-story window. I didn't know where to go. I was sittin' up there, I said, *oh shit!* When we got through playing I went downstairs, I didn't say nothing. I got back into Kansas City, and I went into the Cherry Blossom. Mr. Basie, I bought him a half a pint of whisky, I said, you've got a good band, I wish you a lot of luck, I'm gonna get my drums and get my stuff together, and I'm going back to Omaha, Nebraska, to finish my schoolin'. That's when they *[Ben Webster, Joe Keyes, and Page]* put me in the shit house!

There was a tavern down on the corner, and you could go in the back, you could go in the toilet, them boys done broke the case, and Joe Keyes was coming out with quarts of whisky. When they'd try to convince me I should go with Basie's band, Big 'Un would leave, and he'd go out and get a bottle. That would leave me with two of 'em in there. When that bottle's gone, Ben would go get a bottle. I said, I ain't goin' with Basie, no.

I go to the union, with the president and the secretary, and I sat down and wrote a note: "I will join you for two weeks, but after two weeks, get you somebody else." I joined him in February 1934.[3]

They *[Keyes, Webster, and Page]* said we heard about you. You a Omaha pimp. We got a woman for you. You a pimp from Omaha, Nebraska. They got me Pretty Nell. She looked like the Hunchback of Notre Dame! But she had a heart of gold. Pretty Nell!

We went to Little Rock, Arkansas. That band broke up. I said, "OK, Base, I don't know what y'all talkin' about, but we start from scratch. Piano and drums. You got me." I had a little money. I said I can pay your way to where you want to go.

One time Basie's sick. Moten says, "OK, fellas, put a quarter in the hat for Basie." Room and board is five dollars a week. Do you know that four assholes would not put a quarter in the hat for that man? Mr. Murray, this is the fucking truth. And those same four assholes, he took them to New York![4]

THE GREATEST BANDLEADER IN THE HISTORY OF THE WORLD

Duke got the key; he got the key when he came out there. From Bennie Moten, they learned a lot. I broke it down to 'em. They learned a lot. That was the greatest bandleader. Bennie Moten was the greatest bandleader in the history of the world. He was a master. That was the *professor.* They learned a lot from him, musically and otherwise. Truth of the pudding, when we all went back to Bennie, and he had the fifteen pieces, and Basie and Bus, Bus put the chord down, Basie'd be playin' the piano. Bennie would come up on the bandstand and says, "Uh, my boys, would you loan me my band for just a minute?" Sure, Mo, it's your band. And the minute he touched that piano and played one tune called "From Outer Space," and when he hit it, that band *settled.* They'd settle for a couple of weeks and jump again. And he'd come back in, and he'd sit back down again, and it would be just like that. He had that touch. Basie learned that thing, he got that thing, he just said, bam, he'd ride for eight bars.

That Battle of Music

I found out the association that Basie and Durham had. They were like Rogers and Hart. They were collaborators, see? Basie'd come up with the *ideas,* but Durham knew how to *put it down.* That's why the arrangements worked. 'Cause Durham, when he left Kansas City, he took all the arrangements and he put 'em in Jimmie Lunceford's book. We're sittin' there playin' 'em in Kansas City by head. Because when we came in, in Hartford, we played a battle against Mr. Jimmie Lunceford's band. Aw, man, they had on their brown and stuff and we're just a raggedy band from Kansas City, and they play a set—and they playin' tunes we *been playin'* and they reading the music—and soon as they get through playin', we play the *same thing* but we could play it better because we knew how it went—we were the originals! Now that's the one that they all write about—that battle of music—it's in the paper, and the people can sure tell ya they never could understand how a little raggedy band could come out there—and this is the great Jimmy Lunceford! We kicked their teeth out![5] Because they're tryin' to play what Durham had put in the book.

Basie Got Two Letters

This I tell you! We in the Reno Club, Kansas City. These people coming in that place with evening gowns on. This is a joint. The Reno was the joint! Let the good times roll! These weren't thrill seekers. These were doers. When it came to sex, we could have more sex than anything. See, we were trained: never go to bed with the boss's daughter, as Charlie

Ryan used to say. It was four or five cabs out there to take
you to meet a white woman. On the sidewalk, not in the club.

Everything that came through Kansas City came through
Ellis Burton's place for his spaghetti and meatballs. Everything. From Sophie Tucker *up*. Y'understand? One time
Basie gave me a fright right in the Reno. He came in the Reno
one night. I don't know what's wrong with that boy. And he
cussed Sol's wife out 'cause she wouldn't give him a bottle of
gin. He called this woman everything. You thought he was on
125th Street, cussing out this white woman in Kansas City. I
said o'm'god! I said come on, man, let's play somethin'. Boy,
he was in his cups! She said, "Why don't you buy it?" He
thought that she should give it to him! "Naw, I ain't givin' ya
nothing, Base." And he'd cuss her out. That's the boss's wife!
And when little Sol came in and said, "Aw, Basie, what's the
matter? Oh, all right," he went and got him a bottle.

One time Basie went downstairs to talk to the manager,
and Jimmy Rushing called some tunes. The band blew the
dessert off the people's tables! The man said, *get out!* We
blasted them people off there. See, Basie never had a loud
band. We don't play loud. I said, Basie, never use that piano
mike. Freddie Green don't have no microphone, but you can
hear from here to New Jersey, thanks to Mr. Walter Page.
He taught us. He was the key to the rhythm section, not me.

We in the Reno. Basie got two letters. He's got a letter
from Charlie Barnet and he's got a letter from John Hammond. He sat down and read them. I said, Base, this is the
one you answer, it's John Hammond's, 'cause Charlie will
only *use you* and your band.[6] He had never seen this before.
I had seen this. John Hammond came out to Kansas City
and came in the hotel, looking for Basie, but he came to my
room. I said, John, you frighten me. You're the great white
father of the colored people? I said what about your grandfather, the Kentucky colonel, had slaves and all that?

We come in the world with nothing, we go out with nothing. Some people do good because they know better. Some people do bad because they don't know any better. Constructively, of course, the man has been a very, very good driving force. And during that period, because John had started a wedge with Benny Goodman, that was on one half of the page. Now, you gotta get the other side of the ledger. Let's face it: there's black and white. That's where Basie came in, do you understand? So what was doing at that particualr time: trying to get this cohesion together between music and sports and we were the guniea pigs to do things that no black artists had ever done in life. He had the personnel.

When Basie got the five hundred dollars from John Hammond, it's another inbetween, we go into the Grand Terrace in Chicago, and Fletcher Henderson's playing there, and we sitting out, ringside. Fletcher walked over to say, "Want to sit in, Basie?" I said he's not gonna sit in the band, he's gonna come in here with a band of his own! That's *July* 1936. Fletcher laughed. I said he'll be in here — with fourteen pieces. He did! I said, but Fletcher, you sold your birthright. He looked at me. I said, he did! He sold everything to Benny Goodman so he could buy the chorus girl a mink coat![7]

We got in the Grand Terrace, they did everything wrong. But somebody saved us. One girl cussed out Ed Fox. We was on our way back to Kansas City. Alma Turner had an act she used to do with a chair. They brought music for a symphony. So she said, "Why you 'spect these people to play this?" With bassoons, oboes. "You didn't do that to Earl Hines, you didn't do that to Fletcher. Why you wanna do that to these people? You want a symphony orchestra? *Go downtown and get one!*" Alma Turner, right out of Buffalo. She cussed that man out. That's how we stayed at the Grand Terrace.[8] And they wouldn't let us play our tunes. But we played stocks. All the tunes that we had played, that Lunceford and Andy Kirk had recorded for Decca, we couldn't play them on the air. After the air was off, we played our hits. We couldn't play "Moten Swing." Noooo, mustn't play that. But with our background, coming out of Kansas City and St. Louis too, the word got out, and then they begin to leave us alone. But we had such a diversified conglomeration of people from all walks of life. Doctors, lawyers, whatever—we'd been hanging out, and it was a very unique situation to get all these types of peoples. Basie was very reluctant to put his first foot forward, he was always afraid. I said, what you wanna do now? Well, we can go out to California and make a movie. Yeah, we can do that. I'd say, what you wanna do now? You can do anything. 'Cause I told Mr. Basie in Little Rock when they had a meeting and broke up the band, I said, it's me and you. Piano and drums.

It was a melting pot. It's piano and drums. The people that I later met also had association with Basie before me, but they never got as close to Basie as I did. I just had that driving impulse in me to get underneath his shoe leather. And the guys know good and well, the way I play and the intensity that I have, they know when I was on that bandstand, I'm driving, you know, and the moral and civic virtues of the band always stayed up. The main cogs were Basie, nah, I'll stop. I'll start with Jack Washington, I'll go to Walter Page, I'll go to Eddie Durham, and myself. Jack was the epitome. Somebody just told me, I didn't know he played like that. I said, I coulda told you if you had asked me. Oh yes. I said, don't ask me. Ask Buddy Tate, ask Earle Warren, ask Mr. Benny Carter. Will you take their word for it? Don't forget to ask Mr. Earle Warren: he'll tell you who was the boss of that section. That was the ingredient of the cake, you see what I mean? Basie didn't have nothing to think about! He don't even have the slightest idea—he gone! That's the reason they hire me now to do different things, 'cause if I'm there I have that generalship that everything's gonna be all right if I'm there just for the hot minute. That's the reason the man is raising sand right now, to get me on, said he's got to have me on at all costs because he knows I'm gonna be there. I don't know what they're gonna do after, but when I'm there for that one time I'm gonna be there. See, to be that coordinator, that's all I can do, to make you give me what you've got. I have a way of sitting at my drums to do that. That's where Basie has a way, Basie can spank the baby, he knows what to do.

Nobody's Afraid to Use Them Damn Guns They Got!

I'd say, what you wanna do now, Basie? We used to get the newspaper and read about Jimmie Lunceford, Cab Calloway, Duke Ellington. We'd block it out and say: Count Basie's doing this, Count Basie's doing that. I said, OK. We did it! We did the movies. We played the hotels. What else is new? What do you wanna do, Bay? Well, you see. See my ass. What do you wanna do, boy?

John Hammond and Willard Alexander decided we needed a white manager.[9] So they brought this white dude around and he was sittin' up there in the Grand Terrace. I said, *you better get him away from this band.* I said you look up on that bandstand; there's an arsenal up there, and *nobody's afraid to use them damn guns they got.* Get this *peckerwood* away from here! What? You heard what I said! A *peckerwood!* Nobody is gonna manage Basie but Maceo Birch. When we hit New York City, in front of the Woodside, Maceo got off the bus and made a speech. Said, all right fellas, I been with you all the way, I'm still with you. But the only thing I'll tell you to do: you don't owe nobody nothing. Not one penny. Be yourself. This is New York. Be yourself!

When we got to New York, it was the most ignorant band they ever saw in their life. I used to feel sorry for arrangers bringing arrangements. We put Eddie Sauter back in the hospital at forty-three. He come out of the hospital, came down to rehearse the band, he had to go back to the hospital. We said, OK. We'll take part of Basie's band, cut it up, and go for ourselves. It was very difficult for a Dickie Wells or a Benny Morton or a Shad Collins to get in Basie's band, with the Famous Door and things. So, they look for the arrangement and half of it's gone, see, part of it's gone, where is it? Where is it? Just put something in there! Put a note in there! *Find you somethin'!* They'd been used to playing with Fletcher or Benny Carter—they'd been used to *reading* music. We'd go for ourselves, you know. They didn't understand that. See, they in that school.

NOW, WE DON'T SPEAK ABOUT THAT, WE GO STRAIGHT AHEAD

I was living with Basie in New York, and I said, Basie, don't bring your mother up from Red Bank. She don't know nobody up here; all her friends are in Red Bank. All these people: "How you Mrs. Basie? How you Mrs. Basie?" She don't know them! Don't take her away from *her people,* where she can holla across the road, across the fence and swap cakes. So, she went back. He said, you told me that. I said, that's right! Now, we don't speak about that, we go straight ahead.

I've gone through muck and mire with that man. Two or three times he wanted to give up the band. I said, you can't give it up, not yet. I'll break it up, you can't. I said, you can't do it, Base, you gotta be out here. See, we went in these inside straights. Everybody know good and well that they want to start something with Basie, they're gonna have to answer to me.

We opened up the doors, you know. They didn't want Basie in there at the Palladium. Finally, Willard Alexander would open it up. They didn't want no coloreds in there. See, when Roy Eldridge was playing with Gene Krupa, he had to go in the back. But Basie fought. We was opening up doors then.

I left that band four times. Good-bye! I said I gave you a notice in 1934. It's in effect. Good-bye! I walked in there one time, I got on a plane from Knoxville: Willard's got seven telephones going. I walked through everybody, and I said, put it down!

Basie had gone out to California. The black union delegate was gonna fine 'im. Ain't supposed to be out here, I'm gonna fine you. Artie Shaw and Tommy Dorsey said, *what?* You gonna do what? The man is holding Basie's band up. Shaw is sitting in. Tommy Dorsey's coming out. The only way they're gonna get in the movies is for Artie Shaw and Tommy Dorsey to get 'em in, and he's talking about *the union.* They said, boy, if you don't get outta here, we'll put you in a tub of lard. Buddy Rich said you better go on out there.

The Same Witch That Said You'll Never Be Nothin'!

1936: no band, no job. We sittin' on the curbstone in Kansas City, and Basie's first wife drives by in the car with her friends: "Look at you, Bill, you're nothing but a juice-head, and you'll always be a juice-head. You'll never be nothing but a drunkard. Look at 'em, girls. Look at these two blow tops, talkin' 'bout going somewhere. (Spit spit spit.) Let's go, girls." She drove off. I said, *don't worry about it, Base!* 1936: *no band, no job!* This is the wife, the socialite wife Vivian![10]

We get into San Francisco, we playing at the fair in 1939: "Girls, this is Basie! This is Bill. Bill, I knew you'd make it!" Count Basie, still in love with her, gives her $100. Train fare was $8.50. He says, I'll meet you in Los Angeles. He said to me, come on, go with me. I went with him. He walked into the room. He looked at her, he said to me, *let's go.* He was scared to go. He was still in love with his former wife, the one who said he wouldn't be shit three years before! Basie said, *let's go*. Left her! I think she's still drawing beer out there in Oakland or somewhere. Do you understand what I mean?

He took one look at this woman, that he's been loving all this time. Eight dollars and fifty cents out of a hundred, she's got enough for a suite and some change. Champagne and shit. He just looked at her and said, "Let's go." We went down to the pool hall. Here she come, "Oh, Bill. Ha, ha, ha. Girls, this is Bill."[11] She's a socialite. This is the *same witch* that said you'll never be nothin'!

CATHERINE

It was *impossible* for Basie to marry Catherine. Catherine was with the Big Three![12] There was Gypsy Rose Lee, Sally Rand, and her. That's the Big Three. I said, Base, you've known this girl for umpteen years. She could've married five people with more money than you'll ever see.

But *she* is *Catherine! You're* a *goof-off!*

When he got ready to get married, he got on the train and went on there and got married. I'd known her. I mean when it was *lean* days. Before she left Kansas City, before she became one of the Big Three. She coulda had—so here come Basie. It boiled down to Dan Grissom and Basie. So here he come.

In the interim, Basie was supposed to marry Alice Dixon.[13] There's the picture, in Baltimore, there's Alice Dixon and there's Count Basie. She's on Druid Hill.[14] Buck *[Clayton]* wrote a tune called "Druid Hill." When her parents saw *black Basie,* they said, "Nooooo!" You know how it is, the blue bloods.[15] They said you ain't gonna marry that black son of a gun. Say, Basie, when you gonna play "Druid Hill"? He'll say, "I don't know what you talkin' about."

Catherine don't wanna hear nothing about that shit, 'cause she was, you know, fair, too! But she was with the Big Three! I said, that's it, Basie. Go on out there and marry her.

You Can Handle a White Band but...

We've gone through sickness, health, and wealth. The rhythm section: Walter Page, Freddie Green, Basie, and myself. We get in the Paramount, and Willard was down there with his wife, and and I'm in the dressing room, and he's down there with Jack *[Washington],* and he's got Maceo down there, and they making out slips, firing six people out of Basie's band. Basie said to Willard, "Well, you the boss." I said, excuse me! Mr. Alexander, will you have your wife walk out of the room. I said, why don't you fire the whole crew and just take Basie, if you're gonna write out a notice for these six men! "Well," he said, "we want this in the band, we want that." I said you can handle a white band but you don't know *nothing* about a *black* band—in particular this one! Those men will not fit in here! Not in this band! This is a different kind of band you've never seen in your life and never will!

Since I Have to Go in the Army, I'm Really Going in the Army

The way Shadow Wilson entered the band was this. They sent for me to come down to Washington. So I get to Washington. The Navy Band says look, how would you like to be the first Negro? Stay here, you know, when they take pictures of the band, the drummer is always in front, in the front row. There I woulda been.

I said no. Since I have to go in the army, I'm *really* going in the army. I'm a soldier. I don't want to play. I've played enough. I ain't gonna play "Stars and Stripes Forever."

I got back to the Lincoln Hotel. I said, Shadow, I'm going in the army. I'm leaving my drums here. I said, I don't know when I'ma be called up, but I'ma be called up. So, Rodney Richardson was there. I said, Rodney, keep Shadow here. Even if you have to break your bass fiddle across his head. This was May [1944]. I didn't go in 'til September. I said, well, get Shadow. I said, get him, you know. Shadow wasn't coming. Shadow was so busy going to the baseball games with Casey Stengel. See, if there was a baseball game, he ain't coming to work. Basie's trying to do the best he can. He's got Shadow, but he's running around. That's how he got the name Shadow.

I said, Shadow, you better stay here. Stay here 'til I come out of the army. I said, *you stay!* I said, Rodney, take that bass fiddle. I'll buy you one, I'll buy you a good one. I'll buy you an *old* good one. Five thousand dollars' worth: bust him 'cross his head with it. Oh, man. Shadow was the greatest natural drummer that ever lived. *Natural.* He could play on pots, pans, and skillets and make it come out like ice cream and cake.

I was at Fort MacArthur. I got Henry Snodgrass on the phone. I said how's it going? Now, wait a minute, how you gonna get a *telephone* in the army at *that* time? You ain't supposed to be using that phone.[16] I got through, and Henry said, "I got your sock cymbal." I said, OK, well, you keep the drums. My wife was trying to get the drums. I said, nah, the drums are gonna stay right here so that Shadow could play 'em. I came in to New York, Christmas of '44. I went to the Lincoln Hotel. There was Shadow, Joe Louis, and Whozits Whatzits. I'm on the stage taking a picture with Nick Kenny and Joe Louis, and Shadow was behind me. I got on my uniform, and the man on the air says, "Jo Jones is back with the band!" He's broadcastin'! I got on my uniform! They got the picture in the paper.

I got out of the army February '46. I went down and made one tune, recording with the band,[17] and got on a train to go to Omaha to see about my farm. I said, Shadow, you stay here. I'll be back in a minute. He said, "I might not be here." I said, you better be here! I'll go out and get a Gatling gun on you, boy.

They Had Never Seen Nobody Like Basie's Band

Everything you saw in Basie's band was original. Their own style. See what I mean? The time I came out of the army, I said, Base, why don't you do a Paul Whiteman? He had his office. He put money behind Buddy Rich. Sure did, $35,000. I never will forget that. Then he had Brown-something-singers. That's when Milt Ebbins took over Billy Eckstine. I said, Basie, why don't you send Rush[18] down for nine weeks? It's the Count Basie Union: you don't make it, you come back. There was Buck, there was Dickie Wells. Everybody! Pres, Jacquet. He coulda had eight bands out here. Go out! Come back when it gets bad. It ain't working out there? Come on back home. Loyalty—there they are.

The first time we played the Apollo Thee-ay-ter I ran Schiffman from the back of the theater to the front with an ax—a fire ax—for messin' with my drums. I said, you touch my drums again I'll chop your arm off. I kicked Schiffman out of the pit and sent him to the bar to get a drink. Stand in front of me, I'll break your neck. Basie said, "Well, we just got here." I said, aw, Basie, shut up. We got down to the lower state, the man said he wasn't gonna put up no lights because of Billie Holiday. I said, you touch them lights I'll shoot you right in your ass. We got to the Paramount Thee-ay-ter, here's Bob Whiteman. I say, what do you do? "I'm the manager of the theater!" I said, "That's what you do. The band you say nothing to." We had Stepin Fetchit, Sister Tharpe, and the

Berry Brothers, Buck and Bubbles. You don't say nothing to the band! "Who are you?" Just the drummer. They ain't said nothing. OK? When Duke Ellington played the Apollo, you could shoot deer in the back rows. When we played, the line stretched all the way down 125th Street and wrapped around the block.

We did something that nobody's ever done coming into New York, a new band. They didn't know what the hell we were doing—but they couldn't keep still. They said, what is this? What the hell are they playing? Goddamn! What the heck they doing? They *[us, the Basie band]* didn't know what they was doing, but they were feeling it. Now see, they should've had an inkling when Bennie Moten first came to New York and they did "Moten Swing." The people used to walk up and down the streets *[scatting "Moten Swing"]*. Now here we come with a *lousy tune* that we went on to play: "One O'Clock Jump." Now if we don't play the "One O'Clock Jump," all the music would've been stagnant here in New York. I mean, you know, the critics. Now wait a minute. How many times have the critics said something wrong about the plays on Broadway, and they run for ten years?

You can go in forty-eight states, go in any village, in any hamlet, and anybody will tell you how the Basie band was. If a girl had hair this long or this long, she's got respect. There is no respect no more among the musicians. After Count Basie, there's no more. Go and catch any barmaid that was an ex–chorus girl and they'll tell you: of all the bands that came into New York City, they got respect. All the girls that went down from New York and played Philadelphia, Baltimore, and Washington—that was the circuit, we played that twice a year. Any of the barmaids out here right now will tell you there never was and never will be a band like Count Basie's. Right in your neighborhood, one of the Simmons girls is working at the nice little bar, 135th Street, by Mr. Driver's place.[19] The old regulars is in there.

We had the best things going. "Jumpin' at the Woodside"! Come on, man. We didn't go for the glamour girls. They had never seen nobody like Basie's band. Basie's band was lit up! We was as fly we wanna be, we was a pretty nice lookin' band, but we didn't go for the glamour girls. All these glamorous chicks from the Cotton Club—we didn't have to, they didn't understand that.

People is people. If girls needed some stockings, needed to go to the beauty parlor we'd straighten them out. They'd come to the dance, you know. Sometimes they'd be washing shirts for us, sometimes they'd cook something at home for us. The next time you come back, there's the boyfriend. The next time, they're married! The next time they come up, there's the kids!

Then I got into another scrimmage out there in California. There was two people that held up for me: Tommy Dorsey and Artie Shaw. Shaw just talked about it last September, sat down and talked all about it. I went through a lot of shit. See, there's two things that can bring violence out of me: my wife and Count Basie. Your ass could be walkin', ridin', fartin', shootin', or shittin'. When I get out of the hospital, I'll find ya, I'll kill ya! Don't fuck with my wife and don't fuck with Count Basie. Got it? Every manager that come along says if you can get on the good side of that drummer, you're all right.

They Said The Negro Would Never Be Free

You know, years ago when they had the slaves, the first instrument—drums. Here's a plantation ten miles away. Here's a plantation over here. Welllll. Some could go and visit and some couldn't. All of 'em wasn't Simon Legrees.[1] When they wanted to send a message, they'd get on somethin': they'd send out messages. Don't get flogged! Don't beat on nothin': they sendin' out messages!

Down in Birmingham I ran into some of the big dogs of the socialites, you know, and I told 'em I wanted to go up to look at my old homestead, 3820 Cliff Road. They said, "What? That's Mountain Terrace!" I said that's what I said. I'm in the front door. I lived in a house, I didn't live over a garage. I didn't live in servants' quarters.

Edgar Battle[2] never went in no back doors. Not in Birmingham, Alabama. Not in Mobile, Alabama. See, people don't know nothing about this shit. They think they up-south and down-north.

Jo, We Got a Nice Police Department Here, Don't Hit No More Policemen

We get into Pittsburgh. Everybody else was jumping up and down.[3] I became ill. Everybody was gone. We were at a little Greek hotel and they didn't know what to do with me. The po-lice come. So they take me to the police station to send me to the hospital. They say, "What you doing here?" I say, well, I'm playing with Count Basie, we playing at the Chatterbox. "Count Basie?" Yeah. They say, "There's no colored bands down there!" I said, he's very much colored music, mister. "Well, I know you boys is down there and you gonna be fooling with the white women and you gonna be smoking marijuana." I just got up. I hit that policeman! That policeman: they poured water on him for a half hour. They took me to Mayview because they knew I was crazy. So I got there, John Hammond came, my mother came, my wife. So a doctor got back into Pittsburgh, saw Basie, came back and said, "Yeah, he's colored." They didn't believe that! This is 1937. I'm in the paper! Every time I go to Pittsburgh and walk up to a traffic cop he says, "Jo, get away!" I say, I ain't gonna hit you![4]

Pardon me officer, can you tell me why, in the same hotel, we had to go in the back door? I was there with the saints and sinners, and 'cross the street I had to play checkers and chess with the labor people. They said, Jo, we got a nice police department here, don't hit no more policemen. I cold-clocked that son of a gun. Bap! They put me in a straightjacket, said, "He's crazy! He's playing with a colored band in the Chatterbox?"[5] John talks about this in his book, you know: I'm Mr. X![6] But he lies: I didn't knock out but one policeman!

Boley

I was with somebody last night, and we was talking about Oklahoma. I said I'm going to Boley[7] to get me some sausage. *Boley?* I said never mind. It's a black town. During the

Depression some people said, "Let's go down there and hold up some people." They didn't hold up *them people!* They didn't go down there where *them* black people was!

I'm Up North — I Thought!

Basie takes me down to New Jersey and we're going to see his mother and father in the Buick. It's hot. I said, look, pull over here, I wanna get a Coke. "They ain't gonna serve you." They ain't gonna serve me? I didn't know that! Just pull over. I said, I'd like two Coca-Colas to go, please. Boom. I said, wow, what's that? I said, Basie! Jersey? Georgia? I'm up North — I thought![8] And then the next day I go down to the Alhambra, on 126th Street. The man told me I had to sit upstairs. Shit, I came downstairs and went to Radio City to look at Billy Gladstone.[9] I ain't never went to those theaters up there. Because I had gone through that I came to Kansas City and I walked down to the main street, people told me I had to go to the Lincoln Hotel, the Lincoln Thee-ay-ter. Every time I got ready to see a movie I went back to Omaha, 210 miles. I said what is this?! I didn't know![10]

I'm not going through the Theresa and Frank's and all that, I'm talking about the Braddock — the baseball players was there! The first five black people that stayed in the Theresa[11] — and you can get it on black and white — so that nobody would get it *strange:* Henry Snodgrass! Willie Bryant! Freddie Green, Count Basie, and me: the first five *blacks* to enter into that hotel.

It Is Rumored That Count Basie's Drummer Is Married to a White Woman

They received a communiqué at the time, the time that all colored bands was going to California. "It is rumored that Count Basie's drummer is married to a white woman. There will be no more Negro bands coming to California." Well, we had to go out there to prove something. Places where we used to play: Louis Armstrong went out and played a place, and the manager of the place says anybody gets caught talking to a white woman it's a $25 fine, second time, it's your notice. But now, when I get this communiqué about my wife being white, I go out to Beverly Hills. There's big fat [MCA executive] in his great big chair. MCA.[12] I had everybody in that room. I said, gentlemen, I'm a-just ask you one question, do you know Miss Lena Horne? "Oh yes!" I said I have a permit for this gun. I said the first one that say no, I'm-a shoot him right in his ass. I want nothing but the right answer. Now, she slept in my bed two or three weeks at a time—I never touched her. How many in here, if Miss Lena Horne came in, how many of y'all would go to bed with her? I said, I'm ready. I'll shoot you right in your ass. Who *told you* my wife was white? And why should you boycott all the black bands because it was rumored that—the Negro drummer? I said, don't say! I got it on your ass! I had all the big dudes, right there. I did this.

What Nerve Did I Have!

Did you know I was nineteen years old before I knew about racial discrimination, and when things hit me I broke out in a cold sweat? I should've been castrated! I ain't talkin' about Margaret Sheperd, I ain't talking about Sally Sears, I ain't talking about Wrigley's daughter! Come on, man, I had them broads. I walked right in the Grand Terrace with a white woman on each arm. They said you better not mess with him: that's Miss Kelly's boy. I'm sittin' up there with two white women at the Grand Terrace. What nerve did I have! But I pulled out my pistol and put it on the table—for them bouncers. One would say, "Don't fool with him, man. Before he shoot up the place, he's gonna shoot you!" I'll never forget that.

I said I'm gonna run into a woman that's gonna follow me all over the country. And I did. Sally Sears.[13] She invited the band out to their home, I saw her mother and a man with her, and I said how do you do Mr.—. Sally punched me, says, "That's not my father!" Her father was in New York, giving away hundred-dollar bills—to get some black prostitutes! I knew so much shit!

I had a whole hotel by myself in Memphis. I had a chick that had a Lincoln Continental used to come through the block. Mantan Moreland was down there, Sammy Davis was down there. Burnham, Harris, and Scott.[14] There was nobody there. Everybody, the band, everybody got outta the hotel. There was nobody in there but me and this broad. [Murray: "Why?"] This was a white woman—in Memphis!

But you see, Speck Searcy, who later became the mayor of Huntsville:[15] I used to go caddy for him! And at his country club, he'd take me into *the dining room*. The other caddies are out *there*. I went in with him to sit down at the table *where the members sat*.

Speck Searcy!

The Scottsboro Quartet

Then I go back with the Scottsboro thing—and, oh, shoot, that's difficult. That's the one you gotta get to. I missed it by two hours.[16]

John Hammond—boom—we went up to St. Nicholas with four Scottsboro Boys—he was gonna make a quartet out of 'em. He took 'em to Washington and put 'em on a Howard stage with us, the Scottsboro Boys! We all said, "Oh, come on! Oh, come on!" That *happened*.[17]

One time I went through Decatur, Alabama, and I was laying on a bench waiting for the bus to take me to Birmingham to join Basie's band 'cause I went up there visiting. And a cop says, "All right!" I said, no, no, no, I'm waiting on a train. He looks at me and said, "What? *What?*" I said, yeah, this is me! The judge that officiated there got up and left his wife in the middle of the night and came down there to the colored part of the depot to bring *me* something to eat.[18]

APPEAL TO HIS INTELLECT — DO NOT DETONATE HIS IGNORANCE

I learned years ago how to lock a son of a gun on the brain, so you can do me no bodily harm. You appeal to his intellect — *do not* detonate his ignorance. I have been in a lot of places with that sign: *niggers*. "Didn't you see that sign?" What sign? I'd say, sorry, sir, I've only had two years of a college education,[19] and they always told me that a white man was far more brilliant than a Negro. Will you tell me what that sign says? "Oh, let him go." I had my shit on me. I had my stuff. I went through a section once where there was a Catholic church and a playground, and these little boys were throwing bricks at me. I went right in that church.

Mister Charlie's very smart. He knows who to get and just give you a token. I was out in Southampton, we staying at Joan Crawford's. There's Mr. Pepsi-Cola.[20] First of all, I play checkers. I'm not going to play checkers until you make a checkerboard. I'm not gonna drink your Pepsi-Cola. He went and got a black man and put him on a $75,000-a-year job. I said, OK, I'll drink your Pepsi-Cola. I'm a checker player! Chess player!

There was a time when they said the Negro would never be free. There was a time when they said you'll never see Negroes in baseball or basketball — now you don't see many white folks in baseball or basketball! My friend Madame Therese was looking at a basketball game and said, "Jo, there's only two whites out there!" I said, there ain't gonna be *none* in a minute! I'll be doggone: they said it wouldn't happen. This is a new day. Music and sports saved it.

My Thirst after Knowledge Will Never Cease

I've just been curious about life. And my thirst after knowledge will never cease. Now how in the world could I have a background if I didn't meet a Langston Hughes? If I didn't know nothing about an E. Simms Campbell[1] or you or Invisible Man or something? I came out with Langston Hughes and E. Simms Campbell and then I met Invisible Man and you.[2]

We were on the road one time. I was staying with Basie and Jimmy Rushing, and a friend of mine nearby was an intellectual. So I would go out to his house and read in his library. One time I'm out there, reading his books, *working for all of humanity,* and Basie and Jimmy stole five or six dollars from me! Can you imagine? While I'm working for all of humanity! While I'm giving my *all* for humanity. I pulled out my pistol, I said, I'll kill both of ya. They laughed and laughed.

When I read that clip in the *New Yorker,* when Ralph went down to Oklahoma City and the man was writing and talking about where he come out and where he hoboed and what have you—I could see all of that.[3] I said, oh boy, that's me, I'm gone again! I know exactly where it come from, around Jimmy Rushing's mother's house and everything else. I keep that. When I see Ralph, I'm gonna say, you son of a gun! Touchdown Tigers. Captain Bligh. Come on, man. Shorty Hall.

GEM OF THE PRAIRIE

I love the way this man wrote. The title of the book: *Gem of the Prairie*.[4] It takes you down to Capone. These are some characters that actually lived, some fabulous people that lived in Chicago. Now you read this and record this!

> Flossie Moore was described by Wooldridge as "the most notorious female bandit and footpad that ever operated in Chicago." She certainly was the most successful; she was active in the Levee and other vice districts from late in 1889 until the late spring of 1893, and in that time stole more than $125,000. She once said that a holdup woman who couldn't make $20,000 a year in Chicago should be ashamed of herself. She always carried a big roll of bills in the bosom of her dress and another in her stocking. She kept a shyster lawyer on her payroll at a hundred and twenty-five dollars per month, appeared at balls given by Negro prostitutes and brothel keepers in gowns that had cost five hundred dollars each, and gave her lover, a white man known as Handsome Harry Gray, an allowance of twenty-five dollars a day. She was arrested and released on bail as often as ten times in a single day and in one year was held for trial in the Criminal Court thirty-six times, her bail bonds aggregating thirty thousand dollars. She paid ten thousand dollars in fines into the Harrison Street police court, and once when she was fined a hundred dollars, she sneered at the judge and said: "Make it two

Jo Jones on a Harlem street, late 1936. Courtesy of the Institute of Jazz Studies, Rutgers University.

The Count Basie Orchestra with Dorothy Dandrige on *Hit Parade of 1943*. Courtesy of the Institute of Jazz Studies, Rutgers University.

The Count Basie Orchestra with Ethel Waters, performing in the 1943 film *Stage Door Canteen*. Courtesy of the Institute of Jazz Studies, Rutgers University.

U.S. Army–enlisted men Lester Young and Jo Jones at a jam session at Ford Ord, 1944. The photograph originally appeared in *Downbeat*. One of Young's biographers, Douglas Henry Daniels, calls this photograph "a publicity stunt": neither man was a musician in the service. Courtesy of Hulton Archive/Getty Images.

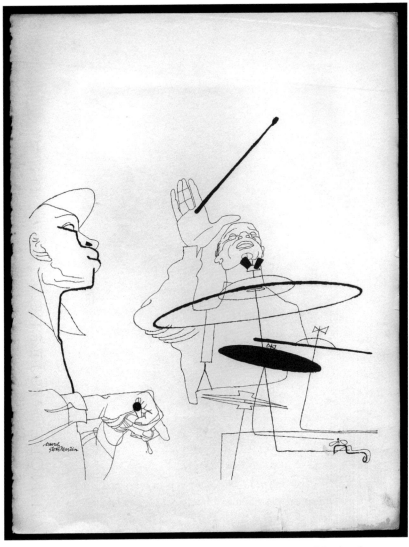

A drawing by prolific jazz album illustrator David Stone Martin of the moment in Gjon Mili's influential film *Jammin' the Blues* (1944) in which Big Sid Catlett, who played drums for the first half of the film, throws a stick to Jo Jones, who catches it and begins playing in one fluid motion, a routine they also did at the Apollo Theater. Courtesy of the Institute of Jazz Studies, Rutgers University.

Teddy Wilson, Lester Young, and Jo Jones in the studio, January 1956, for the recording of either *Pres and Teddy* or *The Jazz Giants '56.* The three played on both albums, recorded in the same week. Wilson, Young, and Jones first played together on Billie Holiday's records in 1937. Courtesy of Michael Ochs Archives/Getty Images.

Jo Jones in action at the Newport Jazz Festival, 1960. Courtesy of
Michael Ochs Archives/Getty Images.

Jo Jones, late 1950s. Photograph by Nat Shapiro. Courtesy of the Institute of Jazz Studies, Rutgers University.

Duke Ellington's funeral, Cathedral of St. John the Divine, New York City. *Performers on stage, left to right:* Jo Jones, Hank Jones, Lisle Atkinson, Joe Williams. This photograph by Don Hogan Charles originally appeared on page A1 of the *New York Times,* May 28, 1974. Courtesy of the *New York Times*/Redux Pictures.

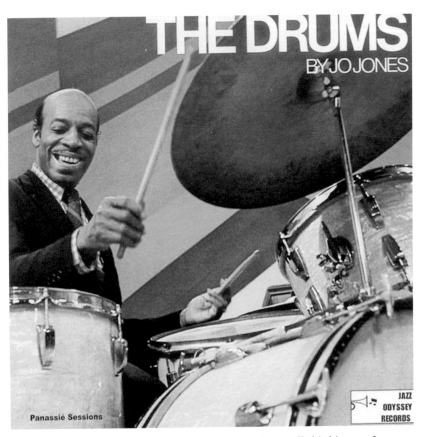

Cover of the album *The Drums*, in which Jo Jones tells his history of early jazz drumming and provides musical examples.

Flyer for performance by Jo Jones and others at Sandy Berman's Jazz Revival, Beverly, Massachusetts, 1978. The sketch of Jones in hat and overalls is based on a well-known photograph from the 1930s. Courtesy of Phil Schaap.

Albert Murray with Jo Jones and other jazz legends in Central Park, July 7, 1973, for the Newport Jazz Festival's "Drum Shtick." (The venue shifted to New York City in the 1970s, but retained the Newport name.) *Left to right:* Albert Murray, Walter Bolden, Jo Jones, Philly Joe Jones, Randy Weston, Max Roach, Art Blakey, and Hank Mobley. Courtesy of Albert Murray.

Birthday party for Buck Clayton, 1981. *Left to right:* Eddie Durham, Doc Cheatham, Jo Jones, and Buck Clayton. Joe Newman (wearing a hat) is kneeling. Photograph by Nancy Miller Elliott. Courtesy of the Institute of Jazz Studies, Rutgers University.

Albert Murray and Count Basie in New York City, 1978, during
the time when Murray was interviewing both Jones and Basie.
Photograph by Frank Stewart. Courtesy of Frank Stewart. This
photograph originally appeared in Frank Stewart, *Romare Bearden:
Photographs by Frank Stewart* (San Francisco: Pomegranate, 2004).

Jo Jones arriving at Count Basie's funeral, April 1984. Courtesy of
the Institute of Jazz Studies, Rutgers University.

The master with his instrument, at the 1957 taping of *The Sound of Jazz* for CBS television. Photograph by trumpet great Joe Wilder. Courtesy of Joe Wilder.

hundred. I got money to burn!" Despite the frequency
with which she was arrested, Flossie Moore managed
to escape punishment until March 1893, when she was
sent to Joliet for five years for robbing an elderly farmer
of forty-two dollars. The prison authorities said she was
one of the most unruly women ever confined at Joliet;
she twice tried to kill the matron, and spent six months
in solitary confinement. She returned to Chicago at the
expiration of her sentence, but soon went east, and was
last heard of in New York about 1900.[5]

She died here about 1926.[6] Can you imagine a woman doing
all that and getting busted for forty-two dollars? This woman
did all that and got busted for *forty-two dollars!* Can you
understand the petty larceny? You steal a ham, you supposed
to get ten years. You steal a hundred thousand dollars, you
can split with the cops! Now these are some actual people.
Read from here, I got it marked. Now I just left Saratoga to
bear this out.

> The Levee regarded it as significant that Pony Moore's
> saloon license was revoked a few days after the collapse
> of the scheme to discredit the Everleighs, an action which
> came as a great surprise to the gambler because he called
> himself "Mayor of the Tenderloin"and boasted that he
> controlled the district. As a matter of fact, even as dive-
> keeper Pony Moore was relatively unimportant, but his
> personal peculiarities occasionally thrust him into public
> notice, and he looked upon any mention of his name in
> the newspapers as an indiciation of power. He framed and
> hung behind his bar, among other clippings, one that de-
> scribed the huge diamond stud which he wore secured to
> his shirt-front with a silver bolt and a small padlock. Pony
> Moore's greatest ambition was to pass as a white man,
> and to that end he applied strong bleaches to his skin, at
> length achieving a pasty gray with brown splotches. He

also tried various preparations for straightening his hair, and it finally became a violent green, but remained kinky, so he shaved it off altogether. In the middle 1890's Moore visited Newport, Saratoga, and other Eastern watering-places and attracted considerable attention by changing his costume every hour, and by the number, brilliance, and odd arrangements of his diamonds.[7]

This son of a gun: what the hell is he doing in Saratoga? When he came in and all the people sittin' up there with the horse, the bays, and what have you. Now he comes in this time and he's got a carriage. He's got white horses: that's a *blond*. Now he'll take her out there and sit down on the veranda. Then he goes *out* and then he gets a brunette: *that's another buggy!* Then he gets a redhead! That's some more horses![8] Now wait a minute. Where are these people telling me about playing the game? This son of a gun played the *game!*

We was opening up the Hall of Fame for the horses up in Saratoga,[9] and all the peoples there and what's-a-name was from Newport, you know, where I stay to play tennis, everybody was there, and I said I wanna find out about Pony Moore. I want to go down to the newspaper stand and find out about this son of a gun. Now this was authentic! And these boys going down to Atlantic City, going to Jones Beach and thinking they playing something?

Now you know good and well: Saratoga, Newport. That's the *thing*. It was a long time before they got down to *Palm Beach* and whatever. Here's a son of a gun playing the game! If you saw him you saw him in a carriage in a surrey with the top fringe. And he's sitting out there with all that junk. Then you see him again: got a redhead. Change the horses according to what he had.

So I got with some old regulars in the jockey's place, to perform, you know. I said, look here, do me a favor. All you people that been hanging out here, tell me about Pony Moore. You get from Saratoga and see that. Now all this is in here.

How you gonna tell somebody about Ma Baker? How you gonna tell somebody about Ma Sutton? How you gonna tell somebody about Pop Henry if they didn't see it? But this happened. They got some fabulous people in there: some fabulous people that lived in Chicago and that nobody know nothing about.

Stylists, Players, Soloists

There are a lot of guys that play music. They are not musicians, they are *players*. They're not artists. It takes a long time to be what you call an *individual*. It took Mr. Teddy Wilson a long time to become an individual. You only have five concert pianists—you got a lot of guys that give concerts. You got a whole lotta guys. But a *stylist?* What's a stylist? There's Louis. There's Fats Waller. There's Lester Young. A *stylist!* A style! The shape of a Coca-Cola bottle, a Rolls Royce—that's a *style*.[10] Duke Ellington? Stylist. He had his chessboard. He had Tricky Sam. He had Johnny. He had different ones. But these things was in a unit.

Everything in Basie's band could sit in anywhere. That's what made the band so flexible—he had a bunch of soloists. The least man in there could hold his own in *anything.* That's what made the band so flexible. They didn't destroy their natural ability. They had enough technical know-how. See, what you got to do, in order to be a good musician out here, you have to *unlearn yourself* of all that you learned. You could go to school and get your three or four college degrees, but when you get out here in the nitty-gritty, you can't be reading out of the textbook. This is reality out here! They take the music away, what you gonna play? Oh, he can read! Yeah, he can read. Now take the music away. Now play. What key is that in? What are the changes? Take the music away!

I've Been a Nut for Reading.
I Want to Find Out.

Let's take some subject matter. Let's just pull one out of the hat here. Let's talk about W. C. Handy. What did he do? Well, he wrote "St. Louis Blues": no, no, no. What did he do? Let's take him from the year one. Let's take his accomplishments. What did he put out here? All that people know about George Washington Carver is the peanut. But what about the potato? What about the synthetic rubber?[11] I say go, go to the library. Get books! Find out about these people. *I've been a nut for reading. I want to find out!* Youth wants to know.

Youth. Wants. *To know!* YOUTH WANTS TO KNOW!

This man know good and well he didn't write nothin'. Sinclair Lewis! She wrote all his *woik*. He didn't *do* nothin' but drink! He din' write *nothin'*. He'd drink. She'd say, "Come here, boy"; she'd straighten up his stuff, and he'd take the bow! That's worse than the Shakespeare story.[12]

See, I was locked up in books. I was locked up! How do you think I'm so brilliant? I have suggested some things that should be written, like the time I came up with the book on Blind Tom and different ones.[13] I've just been always a seeker after knowledge.

I've been around seeing people with a lot of books, and I ask them, do you have so and so? It took me twenty-five years, with thirty people, to get the Rogers series. They had everything, but they didn't have Rogers. "You don't have J. A. Rogers?"[14]

I caught them writers under the tent up in Newport. Everybody was there, Leonard Feather and all of them. They

said, "What ya got there, Jo?" I said, a Bible. I said, you guys
got a Bible? I said, don't worry about it. They had Leonard
Feathers in those days too.

Faith Baldwin.[15] What's his name? *James Baldwin?* And
he's a writer? He don't even know what Harlem—he can't
even spell Harlem! Lena Horne was down the street, and
she said to him, little boy, sit down, what are you writing? I
finally saw him after Sidney Poitier and Max Roach's wife
did the movie,[16] and he comes in, and he's *James Baldwin,*
and I said boy—I got some cats at home that can write better than you. I got some chickens on my farm! I said, *little
boy,* haven't you ever heard of *Invisible Man?*[17] What? You
are a *writer?*[18] I said, I hope you make a million dollars, boy.
I said, now you do yourself a favor, revamp yourself, and get
yourself together. So, he came out with another thing that
made sense. He couldn't write two blocks. *James Baldwin!*
And I went to South America, and I saw some white people
with a Baldwin book, and they said, "Oh, this is a wonderful
book." I said, no shit. I said, hey, you didn't get no hash and
grits *there!* You know!

But in this age of complexity and what have you, we
know what it is, *Albert.* You're a writer, but your inflections,
with the music—you got it. Invisible Man? With the trumpet?[19] He's got it. He knows what it is. But that gives you
oversight that you can write *life. C'est la vie.* You got it. But
it's always the imitator. It's not the originator. It's always the
imitator that reaps the harvest.[20]

I asked some people, do you know where my mother
was buried? My real mother? *What?* Next to Paul Laurence
Dunbar, in Dayton, Ohio. Gooooo see it! *Elizabeth Jones.* Go
see it! Check it out. That man put more language out here
than you people will ever see! 'Cause he could've said this
here, that there, and the other. *Paul Laurence Dunbar!*

I had a bass player I liked. He had a mustache—handle-
bar. I named him Mark Twain. I said, ladies and gentleman,

fresh from his frog hop contest in California, I give you Mark Twain on the bass! I said, hit it there, professor! He said what? By yourself, play anything!

THESE KIDS ARE CONDITIONED. COLONIZATION!

I felt so sorry for Milt Hinton. Milt is trying to do something in his community with young boys. He said, fellas, we just lost a great man today. "Who was that?" He said Paul Robeson, Mr. Paul Robeson. "Man, what did that dude do?" Fortunately for me, Mr. Paul Robeson was a very personal, dear friend of mine. And it wasn't fashionable after *those days* to be a friend of Mr. Robeson.[21]

You want to hear something pitiful? I told Clark Terry, I told them all, Teddy Wilson. Now you go to school and ask, how many people know about Art Tatum, Charlie Parker. "Charlie Parker, who's that?" I had a friend of mine a few years ago, he had Ahmad Jamal, he had Dizzy, he had Sonny Stitt, to come out and play for the kiddies, sixteen, seventeen years old. They said, "Man, what's that stuff, man, we doin' our thing!" And they came in from home with *right on, black power,* they look at Sonny Stitt, Dizzy, like "who's that man"? But—they know Benny Goodman! These kids are conditioned. *Colonization!*

You know what I mean? I did a thing just before I went to Europe. I did a thing that I did with people twenty-five, thirty years ago and they didn't recognize it. They had to go to the bar and get drunk. Don't you remember I was doing it for you kids? I used to hold class with you guys, '51, '52, '53, you remember that? Well, this is the same thing. Now that you got your pictures in the paper, you don't remember!

After I finished giving away the Gene Krupa Award, the next morning somebody had nerve enough to tell me they want me to go down and see the Johnson plant. I said you don't *own* Chippewa Falls. Newsprint! I'm a printer by trade![22] I hang out with people that make the newsprint. You know what I mean?

I don't understand with the books that I've had at my disposal, books I've had guys get to read. Like that out-of-print book: since '68 I've tried to get them to get James M. Trotter's *Music and Some Highly Musical People.*[23] I'm getting more compliments now in the last year. "I got that book!" a guy tells me. I said, well, what took you so long? You coulda got that book instead of going through the block. But everytime I saw you, you were in Beefsteak Charlie's with your head thrown back. I saw you in Jim and Andy's.[24] You coulda gone right down there to Twenty-third Street to get it. "Well, I thought you had . . ." No! I got another place. I can give you an addresss. They have the book. They're not gonna give it to you. You have to send a money order for it. "How do you find out these things?" Because all my life I was a nut. I forget that I was in these carnivals, these circuses. I forgot! I've been those things and I was always a nut.

The Dark Archer

I was down here with Joe Bushkin, Knopf, Bob Constantine, and William Randolph Hearst. It was at Toots Shor's.[25] [Unintelligible] was there and he said, "You know what, something should be done about him." They said, "About who?"About Isaac Murphy! [Unintelligible] got with the boys and put that monument up. It's the most rewarding thing to see how this man lived. "He was truthful, did not bet, nor had others bet for him." He raced clean. "The Dark Archer," they called him, a tribute to the famous English jockey Fred Archer. Murphy's record of 44 percent winners, 628 out of 1012 races, has never been equaled.[26] He died at thirty-six in 1896 and is buried in an obscure Lexington cemetery called Old No. 2.[27] In 1967 his remains were transported to a more suitable site in Man O'War Park in Lexington."

Sports! Go to the block, go to the OTB[28] right this evening, everybody's bettin', and ask the *black* son of a guns, "Who's Isaac Murphy?" They may know Willie Shoemaker, and some of 'em maybe heard of Earl Sande.[29] That scandalized all of racing. Earl Sande: boooo. Clean as a chitlin'! But I got some dope on Isaac Murphy you wouldn't believe. This little chocolate drop: he didn't go in no back doors! Everybody was swoonin' at him. He could've had anything he wanted and was always a Southern gentleman.

The Only Thing I Missed in My Life —

The only thing I missed in my life was in '69, no, it was '70. We were supposed to do a thing and Picasso told me — this is a long story, but short. I can show you the bills. Picasso bought a guitar. When I said I was gonna get Slim Gaillard and Slam Stewart, he said, *good*. He was gonna do a portrait of me to put in the drum shop.[30] Then he disappeared. I have my hands and my sock cymbal in Czechoslovakia. When you go in, it's[31] almost as big as that window. When you go in to see all those paintings, there I am! There's another place in Germany. Not Ella Fitzgerald, not Oscar Peterson Trio, not Coleman Hawkins: there I am! You go in there, you see me! But I earned this. There's a reason for this. I come in the world with nothing, I go out with nothing.

People I've Rubbed Elbows With

DUKE ELLINGTON

The man was fantastic.[1] To know how to assemble peoples:
north, east, south, and west, and in the middle! He was a well-
deserved chef: he knew how to prepare an eleven-course dinner. I defy anyone to take me to any college, take me to any
musicologist. I defy anyone to take his music and dissect it.
Take the worst piece he's ever written, and he'll tear these
Bachs and Beethovens and Chopins and Franz Liszts and
what have ya. Because the man wrote for El Mundo, the
whole world. He wrote life. The other peoples wrote because
of their condition and situation. One was from Poland, one
was from France, one was from Spain — and that's all he
could write! But Mr. Ellington spanned for the whole globe,
and nobody will ever capitvate it.

The man never marched: he was marching a long time
ago. He's not dead. He's going to be with us as long as there's
music. His rhythm saved the world. The newspaper people
said, "Mr. Ellington, what do you think about black power?"

He said, "Well, there was 'Black and Tan Fantasy,' 'Creole Love Call,' 'Black, Brown, and Beige.'" I said, I'll drink to that. These ig'nint people: "what do you think about black power?" Well, it's my music, man!

There has never been a general like Mr. Ellington, from Hannibal, from Julius Caesar, from Alexander, from Pershing, from Eisenhower, to whoever. The man was a world-class general. I told the newspaper people, I said, quote me! But you only get to quote in France, Spain, and Italy, not in America! I said, *the man is a slave owner!* He's enslaved all of us! We're enthralled; we can't move.

He knew how to bring the best out of you. He knew how to take the worst out of anything and bring out the good in you. And if you listen to his music, that's all you have to do is just listen to it: it makes you a better person, it makes you a better neighbor. Until him nobody had ever written a piece of music to make you your best.

Back to Back.[2] Out of 1,500 records, I've only made about five records under my own name. But that's the greatest and most rewarding record I've ever made in my life. It's been written up in every place and part of the globe I've been interviewed. "What's the best record you've ever made?" *Back to Back.* "What?" *Back to Back!* Go buy it, I can't tell you nothing about it!

They always talk about the great artists, 150 to 200 years ago. No flexibility, boom-boom-boom. But when you get to Mr. Ellington, you can just ride with the tide. I don't care if you're a farmboy by the highway. I don't care if you're picking cotton in Waco, Texas, or if you're peeling grapes: you still got to come by Mr. Ellington. He absorbed everything like a sponge, and when he sat down, it was squozen out. You talk about fallout? You talk about the atomic bomb? Well, he just dropped everything on all of us. I'm sorry for the people who will be living for the next two hundred who won't hear Mr. Ellington's music. It's going to take us that long to dissolve it. We haven't got to the surface yet!

The man, all right, so he's a family man. He had a big family. This man had a magnanimous family. It wasn't just his wife, his child. He had a whole lot of little children out here. We all know it had to come from somewhere. He didn't have to be on the road, but he belonged to El Mundo. He gave it to us. He sired a people. You want to get into a fight? Say something about Mr. Ellington. *Mr. Ellington was the epitome of what the world has been seeking all along.*

When the people two thousand years ago used to capture people, they'd capture the best musicians: you play for the court. All the musicians that wrote for the poor people; you can't find their graves. Mr. Ellington didn't miss nothing from capital A to Z and so forth. We are very fortunate to have even been able to see the man, let alone to shake hands with the man. Now the ones that sat on the bandstand and rubbed elbows with him—to us, he's not dead. See, because he lives within us. There is not one night that no musician in the whole world does not play Duke Ellington. I don't care who he is! You know why? Oh, what's that? It's a Duke Ellington phrase! There is not one, from eight to eighty, that does not play a Duke Ellington phrase. He revamped. From Stravinsky up. He made them all revamp their so-called classics. I have met all classical people over forty-five years. I'd say, why did you change that symphony? You see, you see!

I feel sorry for the man they used to call "the White Jimmie Lunceford"—Mr. Stan Kenton. So he made a mistake. He's at the Paramount Thee-ay-ter with Nat "King" Cole. Duke Ellington's playing Carnegie Hall. I said, where you going? He said, I'm jumping in a taxi to go hear Duke Ellington. I said, don't go. He did. He came back to the thee-ay-ter, packed up his clothes, left the band, went to California to a psychiatrist, then he became a psychiatrist. Left his whole band there! Every time I see Stan Kenton I say, Duke Ellington's looking for you! And he goes and gets a bottle of Johnny Walker. We finally fixed him. We finally fixed Mr. Stan Kenton. We pulled him up on the bandstand opposite Duke Ellington. He will not play no more. When you see him he's walking on heels like a punch-drunk prizefighter. Why? I say, Stan, you need to be home with your mother, man! People say you shouldn't say that about Stan. I say, why? I sat in his band and played wire brushes, and threw his whole band out on the street in St. Louis. I couldn't do that with Mr. Ellington. Mr. Ellington hired me for two weeks and ran *me* out of the band! It's OK.

We must remember this. We had the man, we have the man, and his music lives. I'm very outspoken. I can only tell the truth about the peoples that I've met. I had a very, very spiritual rapport with Mr. Ellington. I came back from Europe about three months after Duke's funeral, and someone said, "Were you at Duke's funeral?" I said, "No, but I'm on the front page of the *New York Times* playing for Ella Fitzgerald and Joe Williams there." "Well, man, there were so many people at the church I didn't see you!" How could you miss me! Was I at the funeral! It was a very difficult thing for me to do, to go to his funeral.

We were at a studio in Chicago. Duke says, all right, we're going to re-create the Newport Jazz Festival. I said but, but this is the *Chicago Tribune!*[3]

There are certain people out here that we don't appreciate. There's somebody upstairs somewhere says all right, you don't want 'em, I'll take 'em away. So, all right, Johnny *[Hodges]*, Duke, Ben Webster, Lester *[Young]*, Billie Holiday. He sure did take Charlie Christian and *[Jimmy]* Blanton early. We are very fortunate to have three score and ten. To have the man stay on that long? You have to realize that a year in this business, one year, is equivalent to two and a half years for a nine-to-fiver. That's how old we are.

The man was a legend in his time, he'll be legend after, he's a legend now. Govern yourself accordingly. Every tune that Mr. Ellington wrote out here for us, every title, is trying to tell us how to be *ourselves,* how to *be* a good person. How to treat yourself! Love yourself! Love your fellow man![4] That's *all* he wrote. He wrote for human beings. Now if you missed it, forget it. That's all I have to say about Mr. Ellington. He's not dead—long live the king!

BILL "BOJANGLES" ROBINSON

Mr. Robinson, Mr. Bill Robinson: he didn't have no music when he started dancing. Guys that came along to dance in his day didn't have no music, they made up their own music, people clapped their hands. There was a lot of guys that was on the riverboats. He'd be on there in some capacity. They got them little bands of music on there, but when they wanted to liven it up, they'd toss the hat around and the joker would come up there and cut one. You know what I mean? He's gone. Bill Robinson used to do a thing where he'd go:

> This is the way an old lady used to walk with her clothes
>   on her head,
> This is the way I walk when I'm broke.
> This is the way I walk when I got money.
> Now this is the way I walk when I got a lot of *money* in
>   my pocket.
> Now I'm a-put on my *broke* walk.

Ain't no music! You know? No accompaniment. He did it.

I had to take a gun away from Bill Robinson's head. Sonny, who was Basie's man from Oklahoma City, saw Bill

Robinson one time and put a gun to his head. I said, *hold it!*
Sonny says, "He owes me $7,000." I said, well, put that gun
down!

SATCHELL PAIGE

Satchell Paige.[5] We have had a heck of a time since '26.
When he came to Cleveland, I went down to Akron and got
this woman for him. Had to keep her away from him. He'd
say where is she? She's over there. Satchell would drink a
little vino.[6]

I went to Kansas City when he had his seventh child.
They had the old Kansas City Monarchs, they had the old
Whozits Whatzits. Nobody got one hit offa him—and his
babies are being born! I went out to Satchell's house. He had
a telephone! He had his Cadillac, and he's gone. I come out
with all these people. The Kansas City Monarchs.

Willie Mays. I knew him when he was eight years old.
I'm hanging out with his father. And Clark Austin was
catching Satchell Paige in Birmingham. That's when I first
saw Satchell Paige. I was in Birmingham, Alabama, looking
at this man out in the playground. Then I saw him at Alabama A&M: pitching, playing outfield and first base. Then
they went to Chattanooga. Me? I'm a fool. I went there. I'm
a-follow this Chattanooga Choo-Choo. These are the things
I went through.

What's-his-name's uncle, who bought the baseball team
in Birmingham, I had to drive his car from Huntsville to
Birmingham. I didn't know nothing about driving a car, but
I drove it!

STEPIN FETCHIT

There is no so-called white man can poke fun at himself.
You know, the black man has never been an Uncle Tom. I've

never seen an Uncle Tom black man in my life. He pokes *fun* at white folks.

[Albert Murray: They completely missed Stepin Fetchit. Completely missed him, didn't they? Especially people who didn't see him. Those who saw him were laughing all the time. They were not scandalized because they knew what the hell Stepin Fetchit was doing!]

Speaking about Stepin Fetchit, I was so glad. They had a little program on and they had some youngsters on. And the youngster says, I don't know why they would tell us that he was an Uncle Tom, as intelligent as that man was. He was a devout Catholic, didn't drink nor smoke. And *he put the white man on!* [Albert Murray: *All the time!*]

All these people is talkin' about "I don't wanna do no Stepin Fetchit, he's Uncle Tommin'" and what have you and so forth. There's one thing they never notice: every movie you saw, even in *Miss Beavers,* that had Hattie McDaniels in it, they did not have a Southern drawl.[7] Whatever they had to say, they had a roll-out, like Oxford English.

TOMMY DORSEY

Tommy Dorsey would fight anything. He didn't care. He'd fight a goddamned sawhorse in the middle of the day on 125th Street. Because he was a man! He'd fight!

Back when beaches would buy bands, they had a deportment sheet. At Basie's lowest ebb, nobody ever came within fifteen points. When we played the Sherman, the man says, "Don't you guys ever have a fight?" No!

Tommy Dorsey, Jimmy Dorsey: they fighting on the bandstand, in the dressing room—*on the bandstand!* Joe Bushkin and Buddy Rich were fighting. Tommy Dorsey says, "OK, boys, pull the uniforms off, we got another set to do!" They spilled out of the hotel—they fighting in Central Park!

Tommy Dorsey says we got another set to do! Every time I call Joe Bushkin *[we talk about it]*.

Anonymous

One time we were riding on a train through Tennessee at night. The fellas were playing cards, drinking, what have you. I come in, I say, "Hey, I got a girl in my room. Go ahead, I'll play your hand. Just keep the light off." Well, he comes back in twenty minutes or so. I say, "Was she good?" He says, "Yeah!" I said, "Well, you just fucked a white woman!" He was mad as hell, he said, "You crazy son of a bitch! You trying to get me killed!"

Another time in Kansas City, this guy was learning the pimp trade. Wasn't no good at it. Them pimps out there was trying to teach him. They said when the girl comes up to you, you slap her and say, "Bitch, gimme *all* that money!" So, the girl comes up, hands out the money, and he slaps her! He says, "Bitch! Gimme all that money!" She pulled out a blade about two feet long and said, "Come here, motherfucker!" Them pimps nearly died laughing. They said, "Catch him, baby!" He broke the one-minute mile!

Claude "Fiddler" Williams

Fiddler was a hustler.[8] Always a gambler. And the first night we went down to visit Stuff Smith. So Fiddler pulled out his fiddle. That's the end of Stuff Smith. Stuff Smith's a big man, but he wasn't shit to Fiddler. Shit, Fiddler's up to snuff! Fiddler kicked the shit out of him.

John Hammond brought Fritz Kreisler there. I mean Heifetz. Joe Heifetz.[9] You know, people were telling him "play Little Lord Fauntleroy." So Fiddler's tryin' shit. So something happened. So he said, "Sheeeeeeeeit, fuck this shit, I play jazz, motherfucker!" He said, "I don't give a fuck! Fuck is that? I don't play that shit!"

When we get into Pittsburgh, "What the fuck am I doing in this shit?" Shit, he went on back to Oklahoma, with his gambling and shit. He was making six hundred dollars a night! You gonna sit up on a bandstand for sixteen dollars a week? "What the fuck is this shit? Shit, I'm black. Fuck you poor motherfuckers! Shit! I can cut the dice and make $300 a night!"

Fiddler! Ha! Ha! Ha!

He cussed John Hammond and Basie and everybody else out. What y'all doing? "Let's go back to Kansas City." Fiddler? Shit, he's cuttin' dice games making three hundred dollars a night. Fiddler, man, he's a hustler, he is still. He finally did come in to music, he come in with Jay McShann. He's a hustler, man! He'd say, "Fuck this motherfuckin' shit. You what? This ain't Carnegie Hall!" Ding digga ding digga ding ding.

John Hammond: they was embarrased. They thought Fiddler would be impressed by some violin, and Fiddler had heard more fuckin' violin players than Heifetz! He had just got off the boat. They wanna do that shit, but see, Basie had an ignorant band, they didn't give a fuck about nobody. You know what I mean. But the other people that came here, "yasser boss!" Shit, Basie? Oh shit. And Herschel [Evans], ohhhh, oh boy. He didn't like but three people came to our rehearsal. Mr. Bregman was a millionaire, he let him sit.[10] The rest of the people? Get outta here. Herschel. The most ig'nant band they ever seen when they come into New York. Fellas, are you gonna play that again? Naw, we gonna play another tune. If you ain't got it, too bad, we wanna go up to Woodside. Aw shit, what kind of band is this! But that's how Fiddler got out. When Basie died, they sent Fiddler to

represent the union in Kansas City. No. Send Baby Lovett or
somebody else. Not Fiddler.

LESTER LANIN

He'd say "Jo, is this the beat?"[11] I'd say, shit, no, Lester. Look,
he was a necessary evil. He's still a necessary evil, but he did
more good than he did harm. I'm his psychiatrist, you know.[12]

JACKIE ROBINSON

They said Jackie Robinson would never be in baseball 'cause
he was a football player. They were saying it'll never happen. It'll never happen! So Bob Feller says: I want Satchell
Paige. I said, look, Jackie Robinson's gonna be the first one
in baseball—black. They said Jackie Robinson's not a baseball player! I said no, Jackie Robinson is an atha-lete! He
picks up a basketball, in six weeks, he's gone. He picks up
a tennis racket, he's gone. Now, let me tell you a story and
it's the truth: if it wasn't for Gil Hodges, Jackie Robinson
would-a been out of baseball. He went to the baseball writers.
Campanella couldn't calm him down. Nobody could calm
him down. Gil Hodges, you know, like an army man, said,
BAM! After it building up, all that, black cats and watermel-
ons and all that, Jackie was fittin' to take a baseball bat and
clear the bench out. Gil Hodges just hit him, BAM!

MACEO BIRCH

I first knew about Maceo Birch in 1930 when I was in Omaha,
Nebraska, and he was in Los Angeles at the Lincoln The-
ater.[13] The most famous man in show business was Maceo
Birch. He never took a penny from Basie. He saved Basie's!
Basie lined up with two managers, Milt Ebbins and another

one, Jack Whozits. Maceo had a little school tablet he kept tabs on. He could tell you to a point how much money we took out of West Virginia, how much we took out of Charleston, how much we took out of Kansas—he had it right there.

At one time, to try to get him away from Basie, the powers that be downtown took *him* downtown, and in the *Pittsburgh Courier,* they had pictures of him. The first black man that was gonna be in the big conglomerations of MCA, William Morris, and all that. But Maceo was too smart for them. He said, you're not gonna give me this position and use me to take advantage of Basie, Duke Ellington, Jimmie Lunceford. He saw it! He grinned in their face and left that big position. This has nothing to do with Uncle Tomism. This has something to do with getting on whitey's side. You know—utilize them, but don't use me, you can't use me. Until the day he died, in Los Angeles, California, people used to call him up to ask him things about this business. At the Watkins Hotel, he had a box—they left him money in there. They paid for his knowledge.

I told John Lee, you run into trouble, see Maceo Birch. I told all them jokers: see Maceo Birch. I roomed with Maceo Birch when I came out of the army, February '46. He bought one hat a year, and when he went to sleep in the bed, he slept like he was at a desk because of his leg. He told me, you know, what's fixin' to happen out here: he said there's not gonna be but a few black bands left out here. They're gonna keep Duke Ellington, they're gonna keep Cab Calloway, they're gonna keep Lionel Hampton. But there won't be no—you know? He said there won't be NO. I said how long will you give them, Mace? Six months. In six months' time, we didn't have four black bands out here. That man!

'Cause when I moved in to live with him, he said, "What you gonna do?" I told him that Lionel offered me something, Artie Shaw offered me something, and so and so and so. I said, but I'm going back with Basie. I said, how much money should I ask for? He told me. And one time I was leaving Basie and I went and told him to write my notice out for Basie. Two weeks' notice. He advised me, "Don't make the move." I never made a move as long as that man was alive unless I asked him. He made his money on his knowledge.

When Basie bought his home out in St. Albans he saved Basie so much money it wasn't even funny.[14] Christmas time came around. Basie told Milt Ebbins to get Maceo something for a Christmas present. He didn't do it. I was at the Theresa. I was at the bar. Maceo's at the bar and Basie's at the bar. And they wasn't speaking to each other. Maceo is looking at Basie as if to say, "Goddamn, you could've thanked me." Basie is looking at Maceo saying, "Man, I sent you a present, you could've thanked me." Milt Ebbins walks in! Basie says, "Milt, did you do what I told you? About Maceo?" He said, "Well, you know, I mean." Divide and conquer! He was splitting Count Basie and Maceo up.[15] I give Basie credit for one thing: one year when he went to Europe, he took Maceo. "Come on, man, let's have a vacation."

Louis Jordan was in trouble: "Well, I'm out here man, they got me, you know." Here's Maceo Birch's phone number. Call him up. Bam! I said, *knowledge*. He never took a penny from Basie. He stooooole money from the thee-ay-ters, from the dance halls—and give it to Basie, but he didn't take one five-cents.

One year I got on the bus, was leaving the Woodside, and L. B. Woods came out and said, "Come on out of that bus. You owe some room rent here!" Maceo said, sit down. Maceo took his pencil, and when he got through figuring with L. B. Woods, he owed *me* fifty dollars!

It's just like in John Hammond's book: before Cassius Clay, before Muhammad Ali, I was the first black admitted to the Columbia Presbyterian Hospital. OK? That was a long history. But this man that I am talking about, when he said something, he knew it. See, the Willard Alexanders, the Joe Glasers, the Steins of MCA—they didn't have nothing for him. He got in his car and went to the Savoy Ballroom and picked up Mr. Buchanan. He says, "I got a group I think you might be interested in." He went upstate. It was the Savoy Sultans! Maceo got *that* together. Maceo opened the doors. Do you know Mr. Allan MacMillan? He knows. Reese DuPree out of Philadelphia. Boom. They know.

He commanded respect! He didn't request! He didn't demand! He didn't pay! *He commanded respect!* That's something *else.* That's haaaaard to come by.

He got that Basie band in such a position, even today any of the guys that was with the original Count Basie band, when you walk into a room, if any of those gentlemen are in that room, other people in that room look like dwarfs. They don't make it. Jack Washington, Freddie Green, Dickie Wells: whatever you was before you got into the Basie band, *you became something else.* And we put it out here. And nobody ever put it out here like the Basie band did. But that's the unsung hero! Twice they gave a thing for Count Basie and twice he wasn't invited. I don't understand that. *How could you do that?*

Maceo Birch: the unsung hero of the Count Basie Institution. He was a Talmud![16] He was the teacher! When he got in front of the bus and says, "Fellas, may I have your attention? I've got something to say. I'm not going to say it but once, so pay attention." You get into a strange town that didn't exist: "Fellas, this town: I'll give you the dos and the don'ts." If you went contrary to what he said, that was yo' ass! He wastes no breath on telling you things wrong. He saved it to try to tell you what's right. And you govern yourself accordingly. The unsung hero! His brother was a lawyer in Michigan, Joe Birch. He had a sister.

When we hit the Woodside Hotel, the chorus girls from the Cotton Club, they wouldn't come in that hotel. Maceo

Birch used to go out, and I'd get empty bottles of the best whisky. He'd take it and fill it up full of whatever. We'd get Gallo wine, forty-nine cents a liter. Chicks would come in to see him, and he's the manager of Basie's band, and he'd put that stuff up there. "I don't drink nothin' but scotch!" He's drinking bourbon and rye and everything else. He'd trick them. They'd remember him from being Bennie Moten's manager, and when they hit his room, they knew he didn't have nothing but the best stuff to drink. Tricks of the trade.

L. B. Woods

L. B. Woods got with the peoples up in Harlem, supposedly, and he said, look, we can put in $10,000 a piece and we can buy the Theresa Hotel.[17] They said, oh, you don't know what you talkin' about—'cause he didn't go to the schools that they went to. They weren't fraternity brothers with him. They could've had a gold mine. All they had to do was chip in $10,000 a piece. But they didn't do it 'cause he wasn't on their side of the fence.

Alpha Omega, boom, boom, boom, ding, ding, ding, Elk, ding, boom boom, Masons. He was an ig'nant asshole from South Carolina. So L. B. still wound up with the hotel. And when he bought it, he kicked out all the riffraff and made it a religious hotel. They wouldn't allow us to walk on the other side of the street in front of the hotel.

Big Ben Stevenson

In 1926, when Wilberforce and What's-his-name used to be at Tuskegee, people didn't know that Red Grange took his 77 off and gave it to Big Ben Stevenson.[18] They kept him there so he could give a special delivery. They gave Stevenson ten cents, and he never did graduate! This is deep! Huh?[19]

I've never seen a son of a gun be so *dumb!* Ten-years dumb! When I first met Jimmy Brown, I said, Jimmy, lemme tell you one thing: if you wanna be great, take a page out of Stevenson's book. Here's a man, seven people try to tackle him, they're on the ground, he's standing up. Man, they hit him, seven people. BLANG! They hit him, and *they* all laying on the ground, all hurt. They'd hit him and they'd be bouncing off. Every time I see Jimmy I say, *hello Stevenson!* Robert Louis? No, Stevenson. Big Ben Stevenson!

WALTER PAGE

I just don't understand it. The literature, the books that Walter Page had; it wasn't a diary. Every date, everything was right there. I went down to the house and his wife is sitting there, and the man is not in the grave good and she's got a boyfriend. She took all this stuff and threw it away. Threw all the arrangements away. Just throw it away. This wasn't an *honest* mistake, this was a *real* mistake. All I wanted was the scrapbooks and things, that's all I wanted—for posterity.

Big 'Un was my father and he was my son. Big 'Un was over us. We were not coming to New York unless Big 'Un come. Without Mr. Walter Page you wouldn't have heard of Basie, Jimmy Rushing, Hot Lips Page, Lester Young, Charlie Parker, nor myself.

LOUIS ARMSTRONG AND JOE GLASER

I know that when Mr. Louis Armstrong played a tune that the people liked, he had an encore—he had to play it again. He played "The Peanut Vendor." He played it for half an hour. He'd come on the next night: he'd play "The Peanut Vendor." That's all you heard for half an hour.

Down at this place they got a little guy, billed as world's greatest trumpet player, at a restaurant. When Louis came

on the radio, the customers were at the radio! Who is this
joker making all this noise? World's greatest trumpet player?

The man had to go to Europe for his life. Who did it?
Mr. Glaser. There is so much that I knew about Mr. Glaser
from my foster mother and all that. I remember the time
he said, "I want you to go with Louis." I said, now look, I
could say I'll go with Louis and stay with him for a couple of
years, get my stomach full. No. Let me be his friend, let me
your friend, OK, Mr. Glaser? Leave it alone. From '32, to my
knowledge, Louis must have been taking care of fifty people.
Come on, man. He drew a certain amount of money: phshoo,
out and gone. Send this here, send this there! He'd sit down
with his typewriter, type up some funny jokes and all that.

Mr. Glaser had a house in Cleveland that got raided. I
have to know this, because my foster mother was Louise Kelly
of Omaha, Nebraska. She's in Polly Adler's book.[20] I know
what I'm talking about. Very few people know my background in that particular area.

JOHN HAMMOND

Nobody has with John Hammond what I have as of tonight.
The Booker T. Washington Hotel: Dick Wilson was playing
his saxophone and I was playing my little portable vibraphones. It was very hot. This guy comes up looking for me,
and I tell him, you're John Hammond. I said, it's Basie who
you want to see, I'm just the drummer! He said, "You won't
need those vibes, Lionel Ham—." I said, I know about that!
That's not my intentions. This is just for me and amusement
for the fellas. I says, John, you know, you're a philanthropist,
you know, in your heart. That's when I told him all about
himself, his background. Then he tried to case mine out, but
it was interwoven with things.

I told you, John never uses his money, he used everybody
else's money. 'Cause I've asked him: John, I need $200. He'd

say I only have $190. So I got smart: if I wanted $200, I'd ask for $400. He'd say, I ain't got but $350. I'd say good, that's a hundred and fifty more than I wanted. I used to show Basie that; I'd say, Basie, how much you want for the band? "Well, if we could get $150 a night." I said, naw, you write the letter to the promoter, you say, "Give me three nights, three dates, don't tell nobody, I'll do three dates for you at $225 a piece," and you throw more in for X numbers of dollars. See, you always have to ask for more than you want. He'll say, I can't give you two and a quarter, Basie, the best I can do is give you two. That's fifty dollars more! The same way that I was going back to John. I can call him up right now and say I need $100. He'd come up with $75. That's all!

I said I know about your background, your Kentucky background, when your grandfather had all them *thorough-breds*, them *black slaves*. I said put it in there, put it in the book! You're the Great White Father of the colored people? Shut up, John. I peeped his whole card. I got him right in the palm of my hand. He brought me the book. But he lies. I didn't knock out but *one* policeman. But he did come down and get me out of that jail in Pittsburgh. Said I was a mental patient he was transporting.[21]

We were asked to play a debutante ball. John Hammond wouldn't let us go. We were at Cafe Society and he wouldn't give us the night off. They offered to pay $3,500. Imagine $3,500 *now*. Had it been Benny Goodman? Tommy Dorsey? Yes. That's when I told John, John, you're an R.P.P.: a Racist Prejudiced Prick.[22] That still sticks.

I Often Wondered Why I Was Such a Strange Fella

I often wondered why I was such a strange fella. I seem to forget at this point, as of today, I'm sixty-six. I'm supposed to be sixty-seven, supposedly, as of October the seventh. OK? I was born in 1911, October the seventh.

I don't understand. It just dawned on me four, five years ago. Before that I didn't understand. These guys was my age, sixty like me, fifty-five like me. These guys been playin' out here. I just *know* these people know more than I know. But. They. Don't. Know. Nothing! They don't know nothing about Chattanooga, Little Rock, Sheffield, Tuscumbia, Louisville, Paducah. They don't know nothing about Brownsville, Texas. They don't know nothing about when I was frying lard out there in Casper, Wyoming, during the Depression. Sure do sound good!

I can travel in any village, in any hamlet, in any country—and they don't know nobody! And they over there. I come back, I go to Newport, I'm over here. They're over there! I go to Akron, Ohio: I'm over here, they over there! I go to Waco, Texas. Now if I go to Birmingham, they down by the Masonic Temple, I'm on Mountain Terrace! When I go to Nashville I don't stay on Auburn Avenue, I ain't been on Auburn Avenue in years! That's strange, isn't it? I've lived the lives other people have lived, but they don't live life with me! I'm a *fast* racehorse! But enough about that.

I don't see where Muhammad Ali and Joe Frazier and those people fit with Joe Louis. In Sugar Ray's place you had a picture of Joe Louis, you had a picture of Sugar Ray, and on the wall you had a great big picture of *me,* in '49 or '50.[1]

I had to go and get those little two-ounce bottles. And whatever body of water: what creek, what river, what lake, what ocean—bam, I had about four hundred bottles. This is so and so, this is from so and so river, this is from so and so creek. I'd see a stream, I'd say, stop! Wait a minute! I got to get this bottle! I'd see that name and put it on there and put it in m'bag. Then I collected matchbook covers. Then I got outta that thing and began to get menus! I have menus! You know, I'd go out and come back with menus.

Basie was beginning to go out in 1937, doing the one-nighters. They had a book of encyclopedias, forty-eight states, I got them. I'd take my itinerary, look at it, check with wherever we were going. I'd get points of interest: if it was wheat, if it was corn, sugar, oranges, grapes, apples; if it was coal, iron, steel, I was gonna see. I'd run like hell and go to management. I says, how do you rate here? What's your rating? Are you fifth? Are you third? You know. I used to go down to the bureau and watch them peoples. I'm a nut! Everybody else was off somewhere else. But with my *tennis racket,* my *chess* and my *checkers,* and my *music,* I had *open Sesame.*[2] And then when I met a person, I had a background—at least I knew something about this person.[3]

I used to follow Roscoe Simmons.[4] If I found out the guy was giving a lecture, I'd get my little book and I'd take down one of his sayings. BAP! I'd say, well, hello, my name is, you know, and would you kindly tell me something? On so and so and so and so, you were in Nashville and you said . . . "Huh?" Yeah, I was there. "You were there?" Yeah, I saw you in Nashville and I saw you in Louisville and I saw you in Opelika, Alabama. "You what?" Yeah, I was there. Because I'm a nut! I heard he was gonna speak, I'd say good-bye y'all, I'm gonna hear this man talk!

We get into California, and through my connections I made a connection, and here's a chick, we at her house. Her houseguests were, like, the Duke and Duchess of Windsor and shit like that. We go to a party and there's Bette Davis and she's sitting on the piano bench. Basie rubbed his ass against hers and said, "I'm not gonna wash my ass for a month!" Goddamn! Basie would rather play a cesspool than play in a king's palace: money didn't matter to Basie.

I got tired of taking people to parties: Park Avenue, Southampton. Some people know me: they don't even know where I live. Where you live, Jo? 41603 Harlem? That's on the East Side? There's more shit happening over here than ever is over there! They don't play around over here in Sutton Place![5] My partners: Paley was across the street, Paul Getty was there.

I had a sixteen-cylinder Cadillac. There wasn't but eight in the United States. Al Capone had one. Burt, the gangster that got killed in Memphis, he had one. Then they found out that I had one 'cause they were listening. That special-built Cadillac had everything in it. Sheeesh. Say like, when I was running from Omaha to Minneapolis or down to Oklahoma: I'd take the bootleggers.

There's one thing I always did: I always stuck to my music. You couldn't get me away from my music. They couldn't get me away from my professional friends. I'm still that way as of today. I won't change. I change my white socks and my long drawers. Remember what I said that

Maceo told us? You're in New York now. Govern yourself
accordingly. Be yourself. This is a place where you can be
anything you want. Be yourself. Don't get carried away.

FASHION PLATE!

I know they didn't know nothin' 'bout plaids 'til I started
wearing my plaid shirts, sport shirts. That's right. First one.
Pork-a-pie hats: that's me. Every time I come up—right
today—where'd you get that? Everybody gonna try to get
that! Shoes and things. See, in my travels, I save it, I got it, in
my travels in these United States of America: Dallas, Little
Rock, and Birmingham, Alabama. Dallas set the tone for a
son of a gun learning how to dress. *Nobody dressed like the
black man in Dallas.* Repeat.

No little girl—college notwithstanding—nobody ever
been as clean as Little Rock, Arkansas, with them brooms
that they made, the alleys, the trash: you could eat off the front
porch. You know Baltimore, they scrub scrub. Nuh-uh. All
them little girls, they had them little socks on, in the beauty
parlor, it was boomin', no ashy legs, ding ding ding, I'm sorry:
they lived in the beauty parlor. The black man? You ain't
never seen a Texan wasn't clean. Dallas? You ain't never seen
a musician: you can tell where he's from by the way he dress.

You couldn't go into that department store in Kansas
City. Here was this great big clothing place and no Negroes
in there. I told 'em I don't wear your clothes. I done pawned
ten Hickey Freemans.[6] I don't need nothin'! We took a joker
down there, I got him the job. He became a tailor down
there: J. B. Simpson. He had his satchel. He'd come in the
barbershop and the pool hall, he'd take your measurement,
you know, with the cloth, you pick out so and so. He'd make
your suits, he'd bring you your suits. It happened on account
of Herschel *[Evans]*. Herschel was crazy 'bout clothes. "Boy,   .

you ignint son of a gun, I can't get down there, that's the
white——." I said, yeah, you can get down there! But I
didn't have no sense, I just walked up, I said, *get this man to
make clothes.* "Yes, can I help you fellas?" Nah, I can't help
you, *he* can help *you!* Don't you know black people wear
clothes? You gonna let Matlaw have all the trade?[7] Yeah?
You couldn't get nothin' from Matlaw's but a straw hat and
some seersucker trousers.

When I came to New York musicians didn't know how
to dress. You know, I used to be a fashion plate. They still
don't know how to dress. *Fashion plate!* You notice all them
saxophone players from Texas. You see Illinois Jacquet,
you see Arnett Cobb, you see Cleanhead *[Vinson],* you see
Buddy Tate. They don't fool around. *Theyyyyy are sharp!*

I'm in Your Town When You're Asleep

Peoples that I've hung out with: there's a boy by the name of
Roscoe Engel, he went to Cleveland, track star. His mother
would be gone for a week. I'd go rent a piana. We'd have a
dance, you know, fifteen cents, twenty-five cents a couple,
then tell the man, we don't like the piana, come get it.

I played the Kansas State Fair in 1930. That's when
I become connected with the Menninger Clinic. Dr. Karl
Menninger will tell you now that *his* doctor is Dr. Jonathan
David Samuel Jones. I met his brother. And we used to hang
out. When I got with the Basie band we'd get the Kansas
City six and go out and play the Menninger Clinic. And
every five years I'm supposed to go out and play the Menninger Clinic myself. I'm due for a visit. You know he was
head of the psychiatric division of the whole armed forces
during World War II?[8] And then, through that, the guy who
played the drums, the doctor, in the Buffalo Symphony, he
was at Fort McClellan. See, I been hanging out.

I cover the waterfront. When you're asleep, I'm in town, in your town. *I'm in towns when you're asleep.* I don't wait for Christmas and Easter. I'm in towns getting somebody a scholarship, getting some poor kid some form. When you're asleep! I've been hanging out with Huntington Hartford for thirty-two years. He *is* A&P. He's not gonna let me see nobody go hungry.

The toy manufacturers? They swear by me. First time we came to New York with Basie's band, I was going to Harlem Hospital with Ed Sullivan. Took jokers twenty-five years to find out where I was going.

Jo, They Cut Your Tree Down

They found out I used to hobo. I hoboed with my drums, man! They didn't believe it 'til we were in Chicago once, and Ed Lewis went down to the barbershop to get a haircut.

When Willie Ruff[9] was trying to talk to me, the man says, "Jo, they cut your tree down." I used to leave my drums by a tree—blap!—and I'd go into town.[10] Then I'd get somebody to come out and get my drums. When the freight train would be coming back, they'd slow it down so I could put my drums in there. "You got eleven months and twenty-nine days all the way from Chattanooga on the southern railroad, for hoboing."[11] Not me sir!

Slow that train down! So I, and all them hobos, I'd be out there and give 'em some shit. They'd help me put my drums on there. Slow that train *down!* I put my shit in and zoom and when they got to Decatur they'd slow it down and I'd take the drums in the barber's place or put them in the hamburger place.

I was out there one time and there was a joker standing out there, a hobo, and he was hungry, coming over to me. I took him to Bob's and got him a great big fat hamburger. I got him two hamburgers! And one Big Five, that was a drink, Big Five! That was '28. 1936: we get to Cleveland, I'm playing—ding digga ding digga ding. "Say, drummer, a fella wants to see you." A fella wants to see me? Here's the joker standing between two fine chicks. I said, "What you want?" He said, "I'm gonna pay you back for those two hamburgers and that Big Five!" His name was Robertson, that had charge of all the jukeboxes in that territory. He's got two chicks with him, and he says, "Now, this is your chauffeur and this is your maid—here." From '28 to '36: A. O. Robertson! He was on the lam, down there in Alabama.[12] See, you never know. That was '36, he was still alive in '46, he died in '50.

I did the same thing in Texas. A little white boy would come over. I wouldn't let him sit in the white folks department; I'd let him sit on the stage. I would take the Cadillac, with the pistols, and take him 'cross the tracks, back to his neighborhood after the show. He'd come over in the daytime in the fourth ward. I'd see that he'd get home. I went down to play with Arnett Cobb for nine weeks, and the boy's father come in. He said, you know, I'm poor now, my son is rich. I ain't got but $50 million from some horses and some shit, but he's got a hundred and some odd million, you know what I mean, and I'm a-bring him in tomorrow night. I'll never forget how you treated him. The next night the son come in, I said, "Why, you little!" Heh, heh, heh. At that time you had to bring your own bottle. You bring your own bottle, at twelve o'clock they'd remove it and serve wine. They went out to the hotel, got me a bottle, and I'm sittin' there lookin' at him, and I said, you poor son of a gun, why you treat your father like this? He said, "Well, he don't need no money, he's got horses and shit." He later said, "I'll never forget, when it wasn't fashionable . . ."

Is there an Atlantic Record Company? The Erteguns? I'm the one had them at the Howard Thee-ay-ter, when their father was rich![13] He has a polo team or something? Wait a minute! *You know* who I've been hanging out with. All I do with these peoples is to do something for Albert Murray, do something for the Invisible Man—if I can get their ears.

There are people that can swear by me: doctors, lawyers. Dobbins, at Lincoln High School, was the principal. I used to go up and get all those old clothes from those rich white people and bring 'em down and bring 'em to the office. Dresses, shoes, for poor people. I'm always taking clothes from rich people and giving them to poor people. I did it in San Juan, I did it in South America, and I'm still doing it. Dobbins's daughter saw me in California and said, "You're a remarkable man." I said, I ain't nothin'! I didn't have any money! These people had money! I was spending their money! See, I'm a nut. The harder they are, the bigger they fall. *I don't allow nobody to treat me how they can't treat you.*

These Are Things People Don't Know Nothin' About

I went by a private cemetary. I'm with Kid Yella in West Memphis. He had thirteen graves out there. I was scared to play him in checkers because if I won—or lost—I didn't know what to do. Because I wasn't drinking then, I wasn't drinking nothing then. I said, Kid Yella, come on, you know. If you didn't drink with him, he'd blow your brains out! He'd bury ya! See, these are things people don't know nothing about.

Dr. Carlton Goodlett of San Francisco: he's a millionaire, swears by me. You want to be a doctor? Boom. The first woman in the state of Illinois that was the president of the enbalming situation, I saw that little girl. I said, "What do you want to do?" I talked to her mammy and pappy. I said, OK, I'm a-send you to Cincinatti. She's gonna be safe! She's gonna be safer there than she was here!

I was doing a thing with Billy Williams, Sid Caesar, and Imogene Coca.[14] We were going to Rochester to play with the Rochester Pops Symphony Orchestra, and this is on the Twentieth Century Limited. I got my drums. The porter said, "You can't put these drums in here!" I wound up with my drums in a drawing room car.

You must remember: after World War II, the Korean situation, and Vietnam, our moral and civic values have been — boom — and the mi-gray-tory influx, and boom boom. The people coming in from Cambodia, they start them off with $5,000. But the Indian is not. The Indian is not!

I love for people to introduce me to John Hammond five times and Leonard Feather twice. You're sitting with me now: I will accept an introduction from some eighty-year-old who is going to introduce me to you. I'll meet you just like I never saw you before!

How can a kid, thirty years old, tell you how Chick Webb sounded and never saw him? They couldn't come out! Not the people we talk about. When I talk about Sheffield,[15] he was out there, he was on those tennis courts. I said, what the hell you doing down here, Sheffield, you old son of a gun? Down there he married Elsie Hill, out of Athens. Then I get to Decatur, then I get into Huntsville.

Printing Is My Trade. Journalism Is My Vocation.

This is '35. The man with the Denver paper says that there will be another black champion. We go to Coloraydo Springs to play a one-nighter. I go in the haberdashery store, 'cause I was sharp, you know. I tell the man we'll have a black heavyweight champion. I bet this man double or nothing. When the *Denver Post* used to be printed, every day you had to mention Joe Louis's name. I had known Joe. I had known about Joe from Detroit. I said this is gonna be your next . . . He said, "Naw, they ain't gonna let no Negroes." I came out with Tiger Jack Payne. They wouldn't let him be the light heavyweight champion—he had to go to Australia to do it. *Tiger Jack.* I'd come through Canada Lee, when he lost his eye and became an actor—in Omaha! I came out with Preston Love's brothers. "Naw, they ain't gonna let no Negro, they'll never do that." I cussed them people out. *I cussed all black newspapers out from 1926 up to now!*

Pittsburgh Courier. I knew who had the *Pittsburgh Courier.* The man was down in West Virginia: whitey. "They said, what do you know?" I know everything! They say, "You know Ralph McGill?" Look, Victor H. Hanson was my benefactor: *Birmingham News and Age-Herald.* I met Lord Beaverbook in 1923.[16] *Hey man,* printing is my trade! Journalism is my vocation!

Remember when I was telling you I want to recapitulate? I want to go to the 81 Thee-ay-ter? And also, when I'm there, you and I: we going to Tuskegee. See, because don't nobody know what we're talking 'bout until you have the tape recorder and the camera and say now look. You remember I came down there with Jacquet's band. I told the cameras: we have to go down there and see where George Washington Carver lived. Teddy Wilson's wife was there. So I say, look, get those inscriptions there. You're here. Get these inscriptions.[17] Get these down, get it in your book. You're getting history here, to find out about a Booker T. I say you got to find out about R. R. Moton. You gotta find out about William Hooper Councill.[18]

I told my sister when I was fourteen and she was sixteen: I said if you ever become a colored mammy, I'll kill ya. I scuffled out here so that she could get two college degrees. I said the only children you'll take care of is your own! Unless you're a governess. My sister almost got three college degrees, y'understand? Nuh-uh! I just couldn't see my sister with one of them bandanas on, that wasn't it. I scuffled! And the girls on the show, they would go and shop for my sister, the dress, the shoes, and I sent her a box, I sent her money, every weekend. I *meant* that she wouldn't. My sister was the dieticianist for three years in the Merit Cafeteria System, like Horn and Hardart, until the pneumonia boom set in. She was the only one black. That's my sister in New Jersey.[19] See, I know what I'm talking about.

Last year I'm on the grounds and Haywood Henry walks up and says this is our fiftieth anniversary.[20] We want to speak about you. In the gym class, I never knew if I could beat him or he could beat me, and we too old to try it now. He'd fight anybody, anywhere, Alabama, Texas, Georgia, Tennesee. He didn't care nothing 'bout nobody. He'd go up the side of a son of a gun's head anywhere. He said he's a reformed sinner now that he came out of the army.

Albert, you know, somebody made a mistake. They're gonna find my roots. What happened to me between 1926 and '36? Now, they got books on every musician. But when it gets to me—I'm Topsy—I was just born![21] "He joined Basie in '35 or '36." It's a damned lie, I joined him in '34. But what was I doing from '25 up to that time? It's a void! Get fifty books, they'll tell you about every musician, where he was born, what school he went to, who he played with. When they get to me, they stop! I'll tell you why they stop. Several years ago somebody got personal with me. They wanted to know my background. I said take your pencil and paper, check this, check this, check that, check that. I'll give you an address in Washington, D.C., and with a self-addressed stamped envelope you can get all of me from the year one. But you ain't gonna like what you read! I bet you ain't gonna print it because I might be in your closet! You know what I mean? I got the key.

My curiosity got the best of me. I always want to know the background and the history. I knew more history about the guys than they knew about themselves 'cause I could remember. When I'd go out during the day, what I used to do, whatever I did during the day, I'd come back and I'd write everything that happened. That's what I did.

Like Sugar Ray used to do. *Fight.* After the fight, leave him alone for ten minutes, nobody come near him, he'd sit in the corner and he'd fight that fight all over again. Then he'd get a rub down, you know, boom, and he'd take some medicine, but you didn't come in his dressing room when he fought, you know, everybody come in the dressing room—no, no—he went right in the dressing room, he sat right in that corner[22] and fought the fight all over again.

I had a farm outside of Omaha, twenty-one acres. At hog-killing time I'd be out there, ten-degree weather, making a fire from sticks and twigs, with a can of salt—fresh chitlins!

The best meal I ever had was in Holly Springs. Right outside of Holly Springs. It was rice, sweetened water, cold water biscuits, and a strip of white meat. And I had fifty dollars in my pocket. And I was hoboing. This old lady fixed that for me. It was the best meal I've ever eaten in my life. And she had some jelly too. Grape jelly. I said the biscuits, the white rice, just plain rice, and the water with the sugar in it: boom: she got it out of the spring. I said what I can I do for you? I chopped some wood for her, you know what I mean.

I got some cards to put out. They say, "There's nothing wrong with the music business or our personal lives that we can't cure ourselves." On the other side it says, "Did you help somebody today?" When you go out the door, you turn it over, and you read it. Don't help somebody that you *know, Albert.* Help somebody! Just a little thing, if a woman drops an umbrella—here.

Afterword
The Persistence of Papa Jo Jones

PHIL SCHAAP

Jo Jones wanted his story told in his own words and handled his way. Papa Jo was arrogant enough to think and assert that his memoirs could always be assembled—even after his death and in the absence of any manuscript. "It's in The Archives!" Jo would often exclaim, a parallel to Casey Stengel's frequent summary that "you could look it up." This book has proven Papa Jo right.

That it was in the archives, or his belief that it was, comforted Jo Jones during his later years. By the late 1960s, Jo Jones was burdened by the declining impact of jazz on American society and by the growing absence of jazz in the American music scene. Around this time, Jo Jones could be heard saying, with quite a bit of bite, "It's over!" This practice became even more frequent after the death of Coleman Hawkins on May 19, 1969.

But it wasn't over. At jazz's economic nadir, a smallish revival occurred, and with it came an unprecedented reverence for the music and its Afro-American roots. Jo Jones understood this well and quickly: he should have, as he had

111

been working hard to make it happen since the end of the swing era.

Since the late 1940s, Jo Jones had been nurturing the jazz tradition as an oral historian and teacher by greeting every newly arrived musician with his unique lecture—part admonishment, part cheerleading—on the gospel of jazz and the responsibilities of a musician. By the 1950s, Papa Jo was expanding his jazz evangelism to enthusiasts, centering that attention on the younger set. By the early 1970s, it was paying off, and Papa Jo was no longer a lone Johnny Appleseed in the matter.

Working with John Hammond

This development led Jo Jones to seriously contemplate writing his autobiography. He thought that the famed talent scout and producer John Hammond might be helpful to him in this endeavor. They had a rapport, but there was great ambiguity in their relationship. Hammond understood and favored Jo Jones's musical gifts to the point where he was willing to label Papa Jo jazz's greatest drummer. Hammond also recognized Jo Jones's intelligence and was probably aware of how extremely well read Jo was. He was taken with the magnitude and scope of Jo's intellect and in awe of his musical genius.

In the 1930s, Hammond had been looking for precisely this confluence in selecting a black jazz musician to challenge racism by displaying greatness, but Jo Jones never made Hammond's A-list. Benny Carter and Bennie Morton were on it initially; ultimately, Teddy Wilson became the central figure: Teddy Wilson is to John Hammond as Jackie Robinson is to Branch Rickey.

Time line is important here. Hammond had largely put his eggs in Wilson's basket before he was fully aware of Jo Jones. The larger issue, however, is that Hammond was nervous, even fearful, of Jo's volatility. Hammond never got over Jo's outbursts when the Count Basie Orchestra played Pittsburgh in early 1937. Jo Jones is the notorious Mr. X in Hammond's autobiography. After Hammond's book was published, Jo Jones came across a clothing store named Mr. X and obtained several of their shopping bags prominently labeled "Mr. X." Toward the end of Jo's active life, these bags often replaced the businessman's attaché in holding Jo's newspapers, sardines, wire brushes, and ballet slippers. Jo was much closer to Hammond than Billie Holiday and Lester Young were, but not nearly as close as Count Basie.

Whatever the degree of warmth they felt toward each other, Hammond was a logical, arguably the most logical, person for Jo Jones to approach about publishing his memoirs. Hammond was connected—he was the great-great-grandson of Commodore Vanderbilt, who had died the richest man in the world, and he was the "grand old man" of the jazz record business. Hammond was already in a prime position for the emerging jazz revival of the 1970s. An executive at Columbia Records, Hammond was leading the label in an ambitious reissue project of their Jazz Age and especially swing era treasures that would be named the John Hammond Collection.

The concept of a joint and mutually beneficial effort by Hammond and Jo Jones working together on jazz's legacy in the early 1970s went something along these lines: Jo Jones made himself available for a range of informal interviews where the questions mostly pertained to specific reissue projects such as *Count Basie: Super Chief* and the *Lester Young Story*. At least some and perhaps all of these discussions were recorded. The thought existed, at least in Jo's mind, that the transcripts of his comments for the John Hammond Collection LPs would form a nucleus to his own autobiography, a project that Columbia Records—at least from behind the scenes—would be quarterbacking toward publication.

Papa Jo knew, of course, that it would take a lot more to create his memoirs, and he was prepared to do more. The chats with Columbia Records, now transcribed to text for the John Hammond Collection, would be useful, but they were almost all centered on other musicians. Even if Jo had had the opportunity to tell more of his own story while speaking on the record for Columbia, the idea of converting his recorded comments to book form was too new for him to have considered it for himself. At the start of the 1970s, whatever the reality, the perception was still strong that people should write their own autobiographies. The wave of as-told-to autobiographies—particularly sports autobiographies kicked off by the best seller *Instant Replay*—was just beginning. Furthermore, the concept of composing an autobiography on tape as a fast, often relaxed way to write memoirs was just emerging. The technology by which anyone could easily record themselves—the cassette recorder was the breakthrough—was still new.

Milt Hinton and the NEA Interview

Jo Jones had not yet considered telling his own story by telling his own story. That changed, however, on January 15, 1973. The jazz revival of the 1970s was strongly supported by federal funding. The National Endowment for the Arts (NEA), formed in 1965, was giving grants to jazz musicians. The NEA recognized that older jazz musicians, though perhaps beyond launching new and ambitious artistic projects, were deserving of government recognition and grants for their contributions made during a far less fair time.

The NEA came up with the Jazz Oral History Project (JOHP). Senior jazz musicians were given grant money to tell their life stories on tape. Papa Jo Jones, just sixty-one, was selected very early in the program's existence. Most insightfully, a musician—the great Milt Hinton—was selected

to conduct the interview. The recording of Jo Jones chron-
icling his career and jazz's history guided by Hinton took
place on January 15, 1973. On that day Jo Jones grasped and
accepted the shortcut to contemporary autobiography.

But there was a catch to Jo using his JOHP interview.
Both Hinton and Jones, indeed any interviewee or interviewer
who worked for the JOHP at the NEA, signed a waiver
against profiting from the tape and text of their interview. The
grant was to be the entire remuneration. It probably wasn't
as restricting as Jo read it to be, but it seemed to him that now
that he had found a way to easily create his memoirs, and had
actually done just that, he wasn't allowed to use it.

Jo Jones was frustrated, though amused. It is quite likely
that after January 15, 1973, when Jo snarled, "It's in The
Archives," while speaking of his memoirs and his faith that
they would be published or even created after his death, he
was referring to his JOHP interview with Hinton. It should
be noted that Jo used "It's in The Archives" for many purposes and many times. His colleagues had often heard the
phrase long before the issue of Jo's autobiography reached
the front burner.

Regardless of whether Jones could be allowed to publish
the interview's contents, it's mysterious that Papa Jo barely
discussed it with anyone around the time the interview occurred and most likely never mentioned it again. Jo Jones
should have been raving about it. He had told the story his
way, working side by side with Hinton, a major musician
whom Jo deeply respected as a person.

From the 1950s on, one of Jo Jones's frequent lectures
was that jazz people are people and have families just like
everybody else. Two families and family men starred in this
talk: the Hintons and Jo and his family. Jo Jones was rever-
ent toward Hinton and his wife, his daughter, his home, his
work, his work ethic, his secure financial position, his place
in the community, and his value to jazz.

Quiet as it's kept, they made one of the most innovative albums ever: *Percussion and Bass* for Everest on May
11, 1960. It was just the two of them representing music, the
duet, jazz, their instruments, and vision. Jo Jones was particularly close to Hinton.

It seems unfathomable that Jo Jones found any fault
with Hinton in conducting the JOHP interview for the NEA.
It's also difficult to believe that Jo thought his own performance was unsatisfactory. You can hear the interview for
yourself because this federally created document is available
for public perusal at the Institute of Jazz Studies (Rutgers
University, Newark), for over thirty years the repository of
the JOHP's 162 interviews.

There may be more to the fact that Jo never returned
to the transcript or tapes of his JOHP interview with Hinton, but if there is an explanation for Jo's total silence on the
matter, then it would appear to be the disappointment that
this solution to Papa Jo's need to create his memoirs was
unavailable to him.

BLOWUP AT BLACK ROCK

Jo's belief that he could not use the JOHP interview un-
doubtedly triggered his increased focus on the materials he
had been creating for the John Hammond Collection at Columbia Records. Certainly, Papa Jo now realized that the
recordings of his informal lessons, especially because they
had already been turned into text, could be vital to his autobiography. Jo lobbied Hammond and Columbia to help him
with his book, which Jo expected to receive in return for the
help he had given their reissue project.

Columbia Records may never have been informed of the
quid pro quo that Jo Jones envisioned. Whatever was or was
not agreed on, Jo Jones eventually became quite irked by the
absence of progress on his memoirs at Columbia. In a huff, Jo

made a visit to the Black Rock, as CBS/Columbia's headquarters at 51 West Fifty-second Street was colloquially known, and at full volume he demanded that he be given back all his "stuff." Afterward, Papa Jo Jones returned to one of his dwellings—333 East Fifty-fourth Street—with some transcripts of his statements, some drafts of liner notes, and some acetates of the yet-to-be-issued *Lester Young Story,* which came out belatedly in five volumes between 1976 and 1980.

Besides his blowup at Black Rock, Jo also felt that he had further distanced himself from the jazz establishment with his onstage remarks at Lincoln Center's Avery Fisher Hall on July 4, 1975. That night Jo was one of the eleven initial inductees as the Newport Jazz Festival launched a Jazz Hall of Fame. Papa Jo created a significant amount of buzz by using the phrase "quitting hour" in his acceptance speech. The common perception was that in accepting the honor he had announced his retirement. Jo was sixty-three years of age and, in fact, nowhere near retiring. Though he certainly would have preferred more comforts and money in future gigs and plausibly had a genuine interest in scaling back, he had no intention of stopping playing. For Jo Jones, applying the phrase "quitting hour" to this particular issue was a reflection on his being older and having done his part, and on his having helped to raise a generation now capable of taking over. Indeed, he was looking forward to watching them pull the load.

After the event, largely to intimates, Jo explained that by using the word "quit" in "quitting hour," he had told off his host, the industry, and their presumptuousness in creating and dictating just who would be in and run a Jazz Hall of Fame. Jo never fully trusted the jazz business nor the powerful in general, whatever their professed benevolence. Sure, great things were being said on a Lincoln Center stage that night, but over thirty-six years earlier a young John Hammond had said similar things at Carnegie Hall with Jo

Jones a few feet away. The promised land wasn't reached then and probably wasn't close now. Jo Jones felt that his statement about quitting telegraphed to the audience his skepticism and even rejection of a system that had used up so much of his career time in not getting him there. Convoluted or not, Jo wished to revel in the glory of July 4, 1975, while tipping off that he had suspicions about all the grandeur imposed and implied.

The public evaluation of Jo Jones's brief oratory that night was that a great master had graciously accepted an award and had announced his retirement. Jo Jones was positively gleeful that so many had it wrong on both counts. He was sure he had fooled them twice with his sly use of "quit." In finishing his many retellings of the occasion, Jo would shout that he had used "quitting hour, as in 'I quit.'" But in being especially pleased with himself over this turn of phrase, Papa Jo may not have accepted that it was, perhaps, too subtle and that it wasn't even really the way he himself had experienced the event.

That night, privately, Jo expressed a profound satisfaction. He felt he had presented himself *and jazz* with great dignity and that jazz *and Jo Jones* had been honored in style. Soon thereafter, Jo began telling many associates of his perception of the July 4, 1975, ceremony. Jazz Hall of Fame inductee Jo Jones had helped create the art and had performed it miraculously. Every step of the way, he told everybody to "pass it on" and join him in helping to preserve the culture. Now, such efforts were being formalized. On that stage, Jo experienced a moment similar to Moses on Mount Nebo in being allowed to see the chosen music approaching a promised land.

If Jo Jones was choosing to both insult and turn away from the jazz establishment, then what was his plan B? How would he get his memoirs to print? Papa Jo had two irons in the fire.

One idea was to further align with a now more powerful black community, including black jazz musicians, almost all of them younger than Jo, many of whom had been guided in their formative years by Jo. From the jazz world, the dominant figure was Max Roach. Jo Jones also conferred with the poet Sonia Sanchez, the daughter of the schoolteacher and drummer Wilson Driver, who had inspired young Jo in Birmingham, Alabama.

The other idea was to get Linda Kuehl (1940–1978), a journalist and woman of letters, to work with him on his autobiography. In the early 1970s, Kuehl began a determined research preparatory to writing a definitive Billie Holiday biography, in the course of which she tracked down Jo Jones. Jones fascinated her, and it goes beyond saying that she knew no other Holiday associate who was anything like him. Kuehl was wowed!

Rumors lingered well past even Jo's death (September 3, 1985) that they were romantically involved. Jones denied them. He would not deny, however, that the plan was that after the Holiday biography was published, and with confidence that it would be a success, there would be a demand for another book, which would be Jo Jones's autobiography, written with Kuehl. When (or if) this plan was abandoned is not known. After February 5, 1978, and Kuehl's suicide, neither book was possible. By that date, the recorded chats of Albert L. Murray and Jonathan David Samuel Jones were well underway. Their teaming illustrates both of Papa Jo's approaches toward completing his memoirs.

ALBERT MURRAY AND PRESTON LOVE ENTER THE PICTURE

Albert Murray was a pillar to the African American community. Murray's 1970 *The Omni-Americans,* which incisively displays and explains the depth and long-term presence of

Afro-America in the United States' soul, was also a seminal
work to the growth of black presence, pride, and power in
the United States in the 1970s and beyond. The association
with Murray, similar to that with Sonia Sanchez and with
Max Roach, represents Jo Jones teaming with the empow-
ered African American community to get his life's story and
message into book form.

But Murray and Jo's book collaboration represents take
two of the process illustrated by Jo's teaming with Kuehl.
Kuehl found Jo during her reseach for her biography of
Billie Holiday. Murray, who had known Jo well for decades,
first interviewed Jo while he was helping Count Basie with
Basie's autobiography, *Good Morning Blues.* That Jo's dialogues with Murray continued demonstrates that they both
saw the potential for Murray to follow his partnering with
Count Basie by doing the exact same thing with Jo Jones for
Jo's autobiography. This was not to be. Sadly, Count Basie
did not live to see the publication of *Good Morning Blues,*
and, though very few noticed, neither did Jo Jones. Murray
felt he couldn't finish Jones's autobiography without Jo.

This can't be the full story for the delay in completing
and publishing a Jo Jones autobiography written with Murray. In Jo Jones's last years, he made at least two separate
attempts—apart from his work with Murray—to create and
publish his memoirs. Guided to Jo by Sonia Sanchez, Temple
University Press considered and accepted the potential of
publishing his memoirs. Separate from that development, Jo
Jones reconnected with an old musician buddy, Preston Love,
and firmly suggested that they collaborate on Jo's memoirs.

Preston Love (1921–2004) was a native of Omaha, Nebraska. Jo Jones had spent portions of his life in Omaha, and
although Love was nearly a decade younger than Papa Jo,
the Omaha connection provided numerous mutual acquain-
tances. Far more important to their personal relationship
were Preston Love's stints in the Count Basie Orchestra of

the middle 1940s. Though they had been out of touch over the years, the bond of playing together in the Basie band cannot be extinguished.

In 1983, Preston Love was one of many Count Basie alumni selected to play in the Countsmen for a prominent tour of Europe. Jo Jones could no longer meet the grind of touring and gigging, but he was brought overseas for a few featured moments on the tour. Love and Jo Jones drew closer at that time, even sharing a makeshift Thanksgiving dinner.

By this time, Love was more of a journalist than a musician. Although primarily involved in advertising at the *Omaha Star,* Love was building some impressive credentials as a knowing musician who could write about the sounds. Jo Jones turned to Love to be his Boswell. Preston noted that some financing would be necessary and proposed that they apply for some grants. The clock on Jo Jones's life expired fairly soon after. Love couldn't write the book without Jo. Later on, though, Love wrote his own autobiography.

When Jo Jones died, it seemed that his multiple efforts to have his memoirs published had failed. There is some tragedy to the ins and outs of this story and its dead ends, but the greater shame of it would have been if Papa Jo's story was not passed on.

The world is blessed that the book has now been finished. A quarter century after Jo's passing, Paul Devlin took Murray's tapes of Jo, constructed the "lost" autobiography, and by doing so helped prove that Jo Jones was right. There's some amusement that Devlin, the person who finished it, wasn't even born when Jo Jones and Murray started taping.

Knowing Jo

Broadly speaking, I was the proverbial fly on the wall. I befriended Jo Jones as a very young child and remained profoundly connected to him for thirty years. While much has been made of my learning at his feet when I was in grade school, the depth of our relationship and the greater value I have derived from knowing Papa Jo Jones springs from my adolescence. A pat evaluation of why this is so would be that I was getting old enough to more fully learn from this philosophical and righteous man. Personally, I believe the springboard was that I had—for the first time, perhaps the only time—something to teach him. Jo Jones was perplexed by the 1960s youth culture and he wanted to get a handle on it. For this, *I* was a primary source.

I believe that my lifelong involvement in jazz, particularly since the end of my teens, allowed me to retain that 1960s culture's superior virtues. I believe that I was more able to put my two worlds together because of my long dialogues with Jo Jones at that time. There we were, Jo Jones and Phil Schaap, staying up late trying to connect those dots more than forty years ago. I think these talks helped him relate better to his then teenage daughter, and that was their primary purpose for Jo. There is no boundary or way to measure my gains, which included a precious step toward adulthood as I was being taken quite seriously by a genius.

Before that, I was strictly the gofer. What else would I have been good for? The first time that I picked up Jo Jones at Ippolito's to carry his drums and drive him to the gig, I was way shy of legal age, and my mother was the chauffeur. In the 1950s and 1960s, Jo would have gotten more useful help from my parents and would have preferred their company to mine but for one thing: they insisted—as did most—on asking questions. My secret was that I knew, even by the age of five, never to ask questions—just wait and Jo would both ask and answer the question you had in mind. Jo Jones's world-class intellect, elephant memory, and insatiable curiosity would eventually bring him around to exploring your unstated concern. You just had to hang out.

And hang out we did.

Often it was simply the two of us at his apartment. One record on the turntable, a careful listen, a lecture by Jo, a second listen, and then the questions would begin. Yes, questions were asked—but they were asked by Jo, and only then did you get to talk. Then a third listen, another lecture, more listening, some questions, more lectures. Most times, only one record would be played for the entire day—sometimes it was just a 78. Jo and I would listen to a single track over and over again—his lessons were in between the replays.

The *action* was when we went nightclubbing. There was no scene that Jo Jones could not dominate. I have seen people leave the line waiting to greet Jackie Kennedy at the Club Morocco to hear him hold court and hope that he would turn the show into a well-coordinated jam session.

Jo Jones liked to hold court best where the jazz musicians congregated. The stories that he told Murray were told, in different form, a thousand times at Jim & Andy's, the Copper Rail, and even Beefsteak Charlie's. Jo Jones was treated like a king at these places. Jo Jones could ask the bartender— *after closing*—to make a fresh pot of coffee for his underage and sleepy companion, fill up Jo's flask—for free—with top-shelf Hennessy, and—oh, yes, since you're doing the receipts—get a two-, three-, or even four-digit check cashed.

Parallel to my formal schooling were my studies at Jonathan David Samuel Jones University. I took my lessons from Professor Jo Jones in the library that was his home and in his classroom that was the nightclubs. His courses required lab. That put us in the bars, although Jo Jones would conduct his experiments anywhere in the Big Apple. Imagine charging into the Empire State Building on Columbus Day and exclaiming, "I claim this land for Spain!" His courses were rigid, his exams hard—but we had an incredible amount of fun, and there was at times a certain zaniness to it all that was incredibly attractive.

I should add that while I was in college, Jo Jones insisted

I tell him about what I encountered in class. He insisted that I reenact the classroom presentations of Eric Foner, Kenneth Jackson, Hollis Lynch, Dwight Minor, and James P. Shenton. This led to a stunning display of reference works from Jo's library — shelves and shelves of books, including an astounding amount of nineteenth-century literature on African Americans. I'm speaking of the originals! Jo had Reverend William J. Simmons's *Men of Mark: Eminent, Progressive, and Rising* and a number of other original publications on Blind Tom. Blind Tom, much more than any other of the legendary nineteenth-century black musicians, fascinated Jo. I believe Jo had a first edition of a book published in 1884 that I thought was on Blind Tom, but I have never seen a reference that matches it. Jo's library later burned up in a fire. He would show me his books and have me read certain passages aloud. After some back-and-forth, Papa Jo would give me his opinion on what I had encountered in class.

Jim Shenton was a great teacher and splendidly witty. He often regaled his students with tales of his having attending a lecture by W. E. B. Du Bois and even meeting him. Professor Shenton brought early drafts of Alex Haley's *Roots* to class in 1970. But I was being tutored on similar topics by Jo Jones. My guy matched any of Jim Shenton's special guests.

By this time, I was working with Jo Jones. The prime elements in our professional association were the Countsmen, the Count Basie alumni band that I founded with Earle Warren and managed; broadcasting, as I did some momentous radio programs with Jo; the West End, a famed bar to which I added a jazz policy and where Jo held court constantly and gigged regularly with his Jo Jones & Friends.

THE DIFFICULT SIDES TO JO

Tenor saxophonist George Holmes "Buddy" Tate (1912–2001), Jo's colleague in the Count Basie Orchestra, had been amenable to my piggybacking to his gigs since the early 1960s. Often Jo was on these gigs and the three of us—or more— would ride together in Tate's car. Tate was a very congenial, mellow person, but Jo's insistence on being the only teller of their shared stories, the way Jo gave directions, Jo's rules for the gig, and even the general patter of his chatter in the shotgun seat—I admit it was overbearing—came to bother Tate more and more.

One night, at a party for the musicians at my family home, Tate signaled me that he wished to talk privately. I took him to my room. "Do you have your driver's license yet?" asked Buddy. I replied no, but I would be getting it soon. Without waiting for Tate to mention Jo and driving, I added that I would be driving Jo from then on. "Good!" Buddy said, "because I can't stand him anymore."

Later, when Adolphus Anthony "Doc" Cheatham (1905–1997) returned to jazz gigging and soon thereafter took the trumpet chair from Buck Clayton in the Countsmen, Doc would hitch a ride with me and Jo to the gig. Doc Cheatham, who was as mellow as Buddy Tate and, at that time, was in addition quiet and introverted, told me that Jo Jones was the reason he bought a Volkswagen bug. Doc no longer needed my ride, which included Jo's company, and he had no fear that the drummer would ask him for a ride in the small Volkswagen.

I have used the good natures and warm hearts of the highly talented Buddy Tate and Doc Cheatham to bring up the troubling concerns that Jo could be disliked, was definitely feared, and was avoided, sometimes at great cost, by people who actually loved him.

How could this be? Jo Jones was a great man, a musical genius, who did good works for the many he knew and many more for people he never met. As an accompanist, Jo Jones selflessly brought out the best in his fellow musicians. The audience would presume that the soloist and not the drummer was why the music was swinging so wonderfully. The audience would not notice the drummer listening keenly to the soloist that he was driving, nor the percussive responses to the featured player that elevated the soloist's inventions. Jo Jones was thrilled just to have helped the music and didn't mind who got the acclaim. Jo also ran an informal social services program that any musician he came across could partake of. Those activities went beyond musicians and even jazz. Jo Jones was politically and socially involved in the making of many improvements to our society from the Great Depression forward, and he did this all on his own dime. How could he be shunned and even disliked?

I believe Jo Jones's massive righteousness is the root cause to his rubbing so many the wrong way. He was a great believer in the U.S. Constitution, but in his own dispensing of its doctrines, he was quick to take charge of all three of its branches. Unilaterally, Jones would make the laws, enforce them, and mete out the punishment. One set of codes was for the bandstand—Jo Jones would police the gig to his rules even though he was rarely the leader. Papa Jo was almost always right, but his system was wrong.

There is so much more to this.

In the early days of the Countsmen, an entrepreneur was throwing us some prime gigs. Contacting me, this man offered a few dates at nice pay but insisted that Jo Jones's performance be guaranteed—no sub would do. I explained the situation to Jo at the end of a late summer gig. I was only asking if he would be free on certain dates in the fall of 1973. He responded with an over one-and-a-half-hour lecture on his participation in the U.S. State Department Jazz Goodwill Tours. Papa Jo detailed, with his disgust, the official dinners on these tours. The politicians would put out their after-dinner cigars on their unfinished meals, stamping out the ashes on perfectly good pieces of steak. Jo noted that there were starving children just yards from the palaces these dinners were held in.

Then, in a great rarity, Jo Jones fell silent. I loaded his drums into the car and drove to his home. After I had gotten the drums into his apartment, Jo wished me good night and closed the door. Almost always, Papa Jo Jones wanted me to come in and stay a long time—sometimes for days. But not this time.

What was I to think? I was just twenty-two. My analysis—I wasn't going to ask Jo about the dates twice—was that his lecture was his way of telling me that the entrepreneur was the type of person who would put out a cigar on a steak while children were starving. I turned down the work. Neither Jo Jones nor the leader of the Countsmen, Earle Warren, who also knew of the offer, mentioned the dates or this entrepreneur again.

In the story just told, the way it really happened, Jo Jones, however abstractly, comes off quite well; however, it could have played out much differently. When I asked Jo about the dates, he might have asked for the man's phone number and gone directly to a phone booth. Papa Jo might well have called the entrepreneur and stated, "I understand you're inquiring about my availability on such and such a date. I want you to know that I never work for dirty stinking mfs at any time including Christmas and New Year's. Furthermore fecalhead, I am reporting you to the ASPCA. Burn in hell mf!"

Had it gone down with Jo making such a phone call, Jo Jones's disdain for the man would have been equal, the dates would have been just as declined. But the Countsmen, Jo Jones, Earle Warren, the other group members, and Phil Schaap would now have a new enemy, one probably motivated to spread the word that we were the mfs.

I am drawing the reader's attention not only to Jo's volatility but that his anger was often expressed irrationally.

Candidly, there was no fair or balanced system of punishment for transgressing on Papa Jo's principles. He might give you fifty dollars spending cash and a soft "Stay on the straight and narrow" if he caught you stealing, and he might pull out his pistol if you waved to your friend in the audience while you were supposed to be playing music.

You had to watch out: no one knew what minor breach of Jo Jones's etiquette would trigger World War III. I knew though. I knew Jo Jones's loose cannon perhaps better than anybody. Even back then, in my midtwenties, when I was asked what I did for a living, I often responded that I prevented the public from asking Papa Jo Jones for Philly Joe Jones's autograph. In fifteen years, I only messed up once. Dues were paid.

It was the wrath of Jo Jones and my understanding of it that partly explains why our relationship was so separate from my by far more relaxed ones with the other jazz pioneers who raised me—particularly the Basieites. In that world, Earle Warren was my parent and teacher.

Some families have this type of situation. Whatever the love and bond between its members, disagreements or extreme conflicts of personality lead to a situation where communication between warring relatives requires a third party even at the dinner table. In that sense, I have asked every member of the Countsmen to pass Jo Jones the salt.

Typically, on a gig, Papa Jo's feature would be an extended drum solo on "Caravan." After the full band had played the melody, they were to exit the stage, leaving Jo alone in the spotlight. As he would begin his solo, he'd say, "Bring me back something from the bar." Jo wasn't asking for a drink—at concerts and schools there was no bar anyway. "Bring me back something from the bar" was code for "Don't go too far and don't lose track of the solo as you need to be in position to resume playing at the precise moment when the drum solo concludes." As the solo was winding up, Jo—in a stage whisper—would say "George Washington" or occasionally "Holland Tunnel." This meant that the musicians were to come in at the bridge (the midpoint) of the melody and play forte (loudly). If the musicians ignored, did not comprehend, or for any reason failed to follow this coded instruction, then Jo felt free to explode in anger on stage. He often did. Many performances ended with Jo Jones yelling at his band mates, the curtain coming down, the stage lights turning off, the show ending before its planned finale.

At least a thousand times on gigs, I played den mother to the other musicians during Jo's featured solo, whispering into everyone's ear as we neared the return to the stage, "Play the bridge when cued." It usually worked. It actually seems silly that these grown men, indeed, consummate professionals, needed to be treated like children by me, barely out of childhood. I certainly understood why Jones would be angry. He listened to every note they played and made them sound better for it, but they couldn't even frame his drum solo properly—a simple task. I did, and still do, wonder if some of the players goofed on purpose to start the fire.

I remember a cooperative quartet that played the West End who consistently messed up, the Swing Masters Four. Taft Jordan was the trumpeter. Jordan, a soft-spoken man but one who despised foolishness on the bandstand, wasn't really part of the group's problems. But seeing the others mess up or Jo act out made Jordan angry and unhappy. Jones would have certainly agreed that Paul Quinichette, tenor saxophone, who drank far too much, and Sammy Price, piano, the self-crowned "King of Boogie-Woogie" were the true transgressors of the sanctity of the stage. On the other side, Jordan, Quinichette, and Price felt that the wildness of their drummer's reaction to missed cues on the bandstand suggested that Jonathan David Samuel Jones was more insane than mad.

When this gig was first advertised, guitarist Tiny Grimes approached me to reserve a certain booth near the bandstand.

Grimes, who at the time worked regularly at the West End, explained that he was willing to be a cash customer because—expecting fireworks—"you're going to have some real entertainment." There was.

My own parents, who had been living in France, came to the West End for the first time when the Swing Masters Four were playing. Entering the club after the first set, my father noticed a man just outside the door, about his age, who looked quite familiar. Walter Schaap did not ask him if they were acquainted because the gentleman was fuming. Once inside, my father asked who the man by the door was, and I explained that it was Taft Jordan. Dad then said that when he had first gone to the Savoy Ballroom forty-two years earlier, there was a man, about his age, at the entrance, and he had been seething. Inside the "Home of Happy Feet," my father learned that Taft Jordan—the man at the entrance—had just argued with his bandleader, the legendary drummer Chick Webb, and had gone outside to calm down. It was déjà vu all over again.

Soon, perhaps the next night, the Swing Masters Four had become the Jazz Masters Trio. Paul Quinichette's lady, Callye Arter, critiqued, "Some Jazz Masters Trio: one's drunk, one's arrogant, and the third's crazy." Jo Jones announced, "I'm working in a Big Band: one politician and Paul Quin-a-sh*t." Someday I'll have to write of the Jazz Masters Trio's last performance.

There is some entertainment value to making the point that Jo Jones could be harsh with his bandmates and that they often gave him cause to play rough. The anecdotes that illustrate this point continue to fascinate even though almost all the primaries are deceased. A few of my own stories about difficult work experiences with Jo have made it to print, notably in Bill Crow's writing. But such anecdotes must not mask the profound brotherhood and love between all these artists. Their community, a de facto family, plus their talent, gave the world *the* musical gift of the twentieth century. And while the stories might be amusing, what makes them important is the fact that Jo Jones is the greatest drummer who ever lived. That's not just me talking, I stole that line from Max Roach. Every honest percussionist has quoted it, too.

It may be a little late in the book to clarify or explain this point, but here goes. Jo Jones is as important as Billie Holiday or anybody in bringing a new suppleness to jazz's rhythm during the swing era. This fluidity and relaxed flavor in jazz's core ingredient—it is the essence and foundation of the term "cool"—is the lasting part of the big band years. It came from Jo. The specifics of how to do it from the drummer's chair comes from him. Jo's signature is the high-hat. Jones could swing you into heaven with just his high-hat and brushes or sticks or a combination—the purest breathing heard in rhythm to date. Then there is the issue of time: where one was to keep it within the drum kit. Doing it on the big ride cymbal instead of on the snare or the bass drum was essential in relaxing jazz's rhythm. Jo may have gotten the idea from his teacher Wilson Driver, but it was Jo Jones who taught it to the world. Jo Jones was the trailblazer in feathering (playing softer) the beat on the bass drum. I could go on, but this isn't an instructional manual. If you listen to Jo Jones, then you will be a better drummer (even if you don't play), a better swinger, a better musician (even if you don't play or sing), more creative, and infinitely more hip about art and life.

To make that point more personal: Jo is the supreme tutor of my life. Jo Jones taught me jazz, up close and personal, and he made sure that I learned it right.

I offer seven thousand words from my insider position about Jo Jones and his need to tell his story. A reader could challenge the place that I've staked out. For instance, I am not mentioned in Jo Jones's autobiography. I was not essential to Jo's life; he was essential to mine. Being all but the youngest in his sphere, I'm left nearly alone and must assert for myself that he loved me. During his final illness, Jo introduced me to his health-care givers as "another of my wayward children." I imagine I was there as often as Joanna, Jo Jr., Barbara, and journalist David of Detroit; so perhaps I qualified. Whether qualified or not, I was selected to give the eulogy at his funeral.

It was a gut-wrenching experience for me. I have never felt such a physical reaction to addressing an audience. The power of the moment lingers with me to this writing. On the receiving line at the end of the service, two African American women from Temple University approached me. One of them stated to me that Temple University Press had wished to publish Jo Jones's autobiography. She further related that Jo had told her that he had this young man who could help him, but in their discussion it was revealed that the young man was Caucasian. The woman told Jo Jones, "Absolutely not!" A white ghostwriter was not acceptable. But in the receiving line after the funeral, the lady told me that hearing my eulogy, she realized that I was the person that Jo Jones had selected, and that she should have trusted Jo Jones and said yes to my involvement. As I already knew Sonia Sanchez, I find it difficult to believe she was one of them, but it's possible. She was not the woman who spoke.

However, Murray was the better choice when Jo was alive and remains so today. The same would go for Milt Hinton, Preston Love, possibly John Hammond's crowd, and we'll never know about Linda Kuehl. Furthermore, Jo Jones could have done it without any of us. Still, I'm glad he turned to Albert Murray.

This is not a sugar-coated endorsement. I felt that Count Basie made a strategic error in approaching Murray to help him with his autobiography. The supremacy of Murray's

Duke Ellington allegiance seemed to unlevel the field for the Basie–Murray collaboration to play on. It might seem that Count Basie's drummer would be in the same weaker position. But Jo Jones and Murray were longtime friends. They had in common friendship with Ralph Ellison among many other not strictly jazz personages. And they had Alabama, black Alabama. A great man helped a great man create his autobiography. Bravo!

Please remember, however, that whenever anybody chooses to write or speak about jazz, for every three words used, five are owed to Papa Jo Jones.

Editor's Notes

PREFACE

1. Ralph Ellison and Albert Murray, *Trading Twelves: The Selected Letters of Ralph Ellison and Albert Murray,* ed. Albert Murray and John F. Callahan (New York: Modern Library, 2000).
2. Albert Murray, *Good Morning Blues: The Autobiography of Count Basie as Told to Albert Murray* (New York: Random House, 1985).
3. Published in the *New Republic,* October 22, 2004.
4. The chapter "People I've Rubbed Elbows With" obviously owes a debt to Ellington's *Music Is My Mistress* in its organization.
5. Albert Murray, *The Omni-Americans* (1970).
6. Frank Rich, "Freedom's Just Another Word," *New York Times,* September 4, 2010.
7. The piece in question is an in-depth review of the book *Louis Armstrong in His Own Words: Selected Writings,* ed. Thomas Brothers (New York: Oxford University Press, 1999). Murray's review originally appeared in the *New Republic,* November 22, 1999.
8. Albert Murray, *From the Briarpatch File: On Context, Procedure, and American Identity* (New York: Pantheon, 2001), 110–11.

9. Ibid., 122.

10. Ralph Waldo Emerson, "Goethe; or, The Writer," in *Essays and Lectures* (New York: Library of America, 1983), 750.

11. Richard Meryman, "Louis Armstrong: A Self-Portrait," *Life*, April 15, 1966; *Louis Armstrong—a Self-Portrait: The Interview by Richard Meryman* (New York: Eakins Press, 1971).

12. Reprinted in Dan Morgenstern, *Living with Jazz* (New York: Pantheon, 2004), 184.

13. Chip Stern had a similar experience. He wrote of it, in a very substantive 1984 profile of Jones: "I try to direct the flow of Papa Jo's stream of consciousness, but that's a mistake, and only succeeds in bringing him up to full froth. 'There you go, Chip, anticipating. I'm going to tell you one more time: Don't anticipate me, because you don't know one damn thing about me.'" Later on, Stern writes of a cryptic comment Jones makes: "Good question, and like so many others one would pose to Jo Jones, answers aren't readily forthcoming. Papa Jo exists on the level of folklore, myth, and parable; the cracker-barrel philosopher; teller of tall tales; venerable keeper of our oral traditions." See Chip Stern, "Papa Jo Jones," *Modern Drummer* 8, no. 1 (January 1984): 8–13, 38–48.

14. Basie sat in ("Courtesy of Norman Granz and Clef Records") for the tune "Shoe Shine Boy" on the 1955 album *The Jo Jones Special*. According to liner notes by John Hammond and S. W. Bennet, "There was perhaps a sentimental reason for Count Basie sitting in with the group to do 'Shoe Shine Boy.' The tune, which had been used in a shake dancer's routine in the floor show at Chicago's Grand Terrace, was the first tune which Basie and Jones recorded together. The time was October, 1936, the label was Vocalion, and the studio a very small room in a Michigan Avenue office building. That memorable session also was the record debut of Lester Young" (liner notes to *The Essential Jo Jones*, Vanguard Records, 1977). The original "Shoe Shine Boy" was one of the early Basie tunes recorded under the name Jones-Smith, Inc. It is available on the comprehensive 2003 Columbia Records compilation *America's #1 Band!*

15. Milt Hinton remembers, "He was partially paralyzed and

had to be helped onto the stage. He was Papa Jo Jones, senior citizen, and everyone in the house was paying their respects. When he started playing, I could hear the same qualities I'd heard fifty years earlier, and he looked just as regal too." Milt Hinton, David G. Berger, and Holly Maxson, *Playing the Changes: Milt Hinton's Life in Stories and Photographs* (Nashville, Tenn.: Vanderbilt University Press, 2008), 168.

INTRODUCTION

1. Burt Korall, *Drummin' Men: The Hearbeat of Jazz; The Swing Years* (New York: Oxford University Press, 2002), 127.
2. Ibid., 128.
3. I wrote the entry for Jodie "Butterbeans" Edwards (1895–1967) in *African American National Biography,* ed. Henry Louis Gates Jr. and Evelyn Brooks Higginbotham (New York: Oxford University Press, 2008). At the end of *The Drums* (1973), an album that must be heard to be believed, on which Jo Jones plays the styles of various drummers while demonstrating his unique style of raconteurship, he plays the tune "Sweet Sue" with Willie "The Lion" Smith on piano. During a long drum introduction, Jones can be heard to exclaim, slowly and forcefully, "Butterbeans and Susie!" My guess is that he was playing something that would bring them to mind. Willie seems to mishear him, or perhaps misunderstand, and says "Yeah, yeah. 'Sweet Sue,' we call it." "Sweet Sue" also figures in "The Count Basie Institution" chapter in this volume.
4. Quoted in Korall, *Drummin' Men: The Swing Years,* 154. Pres is Lester Young's nickname. This book, with its very long chapter on Jo Jones, is full of indispensable information. First published by Schirmer Books in 1990, Korall's book collects the recollections and opinions of many people who knew and played with Jones and also culls valuable material from interviews Jones did over the years. Korall also cites key information from Jones's Jazz Oral History Project interview with Milt Hinton.
5. Ibid., 123.
6. In the years after he left Basie, Jones recorded several albums as a leader, many as a sideman, a few in a duo, and one as a soloist

(The Drums). As a leader, some of his most intriguing recordings are "A Wig on the Bold-Headed Mountain," "Georgia Mae," "I Found a New Set of Drums," "Bebop Irishman," "Cubano Chant," and his renditions of "Satin Doll," "Old Man River," and "The Way You Look Tonight." As a sideman he played on albums such as Coleman Hawkins's *The Hawk Flies High,* the Duke Ellington and Johnny Hodges albums *Back to Back* and *Side by Side,* Benny Carter's *Further Definitions,* and albums such as *Pres and Teddy, The Impeccable Mr. Wilson,* and *Newport Rebels.* He also made albums with Milt Hinton, Willie "The Lion" Smith, and Milt Buckner.

7. Buck Clayton, with Nancy Miller Elliott, *Buck Clayton's Jazz World* (New York: Oxford University Press, 1991), 85.

8. David Gonzales, "Toe to Toe over a Checkerboard," *New York Times,* December 7, 1991, 25.

9. Quoted in Korall, *Drummin' Men: The Swing Years,* 130.

10. Clayton, *Buck Clayton's Jazz World,* 185.

11. Quoted in Morgenstern, *Living with Jazz,* 184.

12. Quoted in Korall, *Drummin' Men: The Swing Years,* 150.

13. Mark Tucker, "Count Basie and the Piano That Swings the Band," *Popular Music* 5 (1985): 67.

14. Ibid., 65.

15. Korall, *Drummin' Men: The Swing Years,* 149.

16. Hinton, Berger, and Maxson, *Playing the Changes,* 167.

17. Gunther Schuller, *The Swing Era: The Development of Jazz, 1930–1945* (New York: Oxford University Press, 1989), 226–27.

18. Whitney Balliet, *Collected Works: A Journal of Jazz, 1954–2001* (New York: St. Martin's Griffin, 2002), 103–4.

19. Gary Giddins, "Sophisticated Rhythm," *JazzTimes,* November 2002.

20. Ibid.

21. Personal interview with Murray, 2006.

22. "Mose" was a slang term for African American, often used by Ellison and Murray in their exchange of letters.

23. Ellison and Murray, *Trading Twelves,* 97–98. What is quoted here is only an excerpt. The entirety of the letter in *Trading Twelves* is worth reading.

24. Kenneth Burke, "Literature as Equipment for Living," in *The Philosophy of Literary Form* (Berkeley: University of California Press, 1973).

25. "Fay" is slang for a white person.

26. Ellison and Murray, *Trading Twelves*, 100–101.

27. Morgenstern, *Living with Jazz*, 185.

28. I would like to note certain similarities that this quote by Jones has with the last chapter of philosopher Kaja Silverman's magnificent treatise *World Spectators* (Stanford, Calif.: Stanford University Press, 2000). Aside from the obvious similarities (Silverman talks of the need to "become 'ourselves,'" with reference to the artist Cézanne in particular), it would take a short book to explain the shared outlook, but it's there. One common denominator between general outlooks may be Roger Caillois, a favorite theorist of Silverman and Murray.

29. André Malraux, *The Voices of Silence* (Princeton, N.J.: Princeton University Press, 1978), 639.

30. Gail Gelburd, "Bearden in Theory and Ritual: A Conversation with Albert Murray," in Gail Gelburd and Thelma Golden, *Romare Bearden in Black-and-White: Photomontage Projections, 1964* (New York: Whitney Museum of American Art/Harry N. Abrams, 1997), 54. For more on this topic, see Paul Devlin, "Albert Murray and Visual Art," in *Albert Murray and the Aesthetic Imagination of a Nation*, ed. Barbara Baker (Tuscaloosa: University of Alabama Press, 2010).

31. Duke Ellington, *Music Is My Mistress* (Garden City, N.Y.: Doubleday, 1973), 436.

32. Murray mentions Jones briefly several times in *Stomping the Blues*, but most substantively toward the end: "Jo Jones, the most masterful, influential, and enduring of the Kansas City percussionists, is as widely celebrated for the way he signifies with his sticks and wire brushes as for the way he testifies, bears witness, exhorts, annotates, approves, or otherwise comments— not only with his sticks and his foot pedals but also with his mallets and sometimes with his bare hands." Albert Murray, *Stomping the Blues* (New York: McGraw-Hill, 1976), 256.

33. Albert Murray, *The Magic Keys* (New York: Pantheon, 2005), 27.

34. Albert Murray, *The Seven League Boots* (New York: Pantheon, 1995), 32.
35. "Don't carified" means insouciant, cavalier, devil-may-care.
36. John Ashbery, *Reported Sightings: Art Chronicles, 1957–1987* (Cambridge, Mass.: Harvard University Press, 1989), 314.

I HAVE HAD A *VARIED* LIFE

1. Pronounced "Al-bear," with a French pronunciation. On the tape, Murray says, "Do you know the other musician that called me that?" Then after a pause, Murray says, "Duke." Jones replies, with a chuckle, "Well, there you go!"
2. Jones would sometimes refer to the writer Ralph Ellison, author of the novel *Invisible Man* as "Invisible Man."
3. According to an unsigned *Jet Magazine* article, October 4, 1982, Grace Kelly arranged for a new house for Josephine Baker to live in after she was evicted from her Paris mansion in 1969. When Baker died in 1975, Kelly paid for her funeral and offered assistance to Baker's thirteen adopted children.
4. Jones conveys this information in a slightly different way in one of his brief vignettes quoted in Nat Shapiro and Nat Hentoff's *Hear Me Talkin' to Ya: The Story of Jazz as Told by the Men Who Made It* (Mineola, N.Y.: Dover, 1966), 284: "I had gone up and down the country in carnivals, and playing the Chautauqua Circuit. I had done singing and dancing and dramatic skits."
5. I believe Jones is implying that his story is so interesting that it should bring world peace; people will be so busy reading it that they will have neither the time nor the inclination to fight one another.

CAN'T NOBODY TELL ME ONE INCH ABOUT
SHOW BUSINESS

1. This section, in which Jones is quasi-kidnapped and forced to go from Kansas City to play in St. Louis in 1936, is included here because it bolsters his claim about knowing all the ins and outs of show business, including its worst features when it was run by gangsters. Had Jones not made his escape from

St. Louis back to Kansas City, the history of the Basie band (and jazz history in general) might have been very different. Later that same year his big break came when John Hammond took the band out of Kansas City and into Chicago and then New York and the Roseland Ballroom by Christmas Eve.

2. See Dennis Owsley, *City of Gabriels: The History of Jazz in St. Louis, 1895–1973* (St. Louis: Reedy Press, 2006), 50–51: "The place that offered the best wages and working conditions for black musicians was the Plantation Club, the first venue in the city to offer top black entertainment for whites in St. Louis. While white patrons danced to black bands on the river boats, the Plantation was a lavish affair with a chorus line and elaborate floorshows. Throughout its history the club was managed by Tony and Jim Scarpelli. It was a whites-only establishment featuring black bands and arrangers. Surprisingly, Kimball Dial claimed that the Scarpellis originally wanted a racially mixed establishment, but the police put down an ultimatum against the idea." Jones would have been playing with the Jeter-Pillars Orchestra, the band that played at the club from 1934 to 1944. For Basie's somewhat vague take on Jones's time in St. Louis, see Murray's *Good Morning Blues,* 160. Basie does not speak about the Scarpellis, but he does note that Jones was with the Jeter-Pillars Orchestra. After Bennie Moten's death, the musicians went their separate ways. When Basie regrouped some of the musicians, he had Jesse Price and then Willie McWashington on drums. When McWashington got sick, Basie "got in touch with" Jones in St. Louis, and that's when Jones made his escape. Basie's quoted take on this is slightly different (and more vague) in Stanley Dance, *The World of Count Basie* (New York: Charles Scribner and Sons, 1980), 14.

3. Thomas Gomez (1905–1971) was an actor.

4. Virginia Hill (1916–1966) actually died in Austria. It is unclear when she was in Omaha. Jones tells this story on several tapes.

5. This is what Jones called Dizzy Gillespie.

6. Dorsey hired Sy Oliver away from Lunceford to do his arrangements.

7. For more on Garbage Rogers, see Murray, *Good Morning Blues,* 133–34.

8. Slappy White (1921–1995) was a comedian. He was married to Lavern Baker (1929–1997) who had a hit song called "Tweedlee Dee" in 1955.

9. This is said with a snap, snap, snap of his fingers.

10. The question arises, doesn't he know that Murray knows this? Occasionally, especially on the earliest tapes, Jones talks to Murray as if Murray is younger than he actually is. Murray was born five years after Jones, but perhaps Jones was guessing ten or fifteen years. At age sixty, it appears from photos that Murray could've passed for fifty. This is just conjecture as to what Jones might have been thinking. On later tapes, this trend of Jones explaining old-time things for Murray disappears. For more along the lines of what Jones is talking about regarding public laughter, see Ralph Ellison's 1985 essay "An Extravagance of Laughter," in *The Collected Essays of Ralph Ellison,* ed. John F. Callahan (New York: Modern Library, 1995).

11. After Jones says this, he proceeds to tap out the beat for "Sweet Georgia Brown," the Harlem Globetrotter's theme song. After a moment Murray picks up on it and scats a few bars.

12. Vinson, Cobb, and Jacquet weren't the only young musicians whom Jones steered away from alcohol. Dr. Billy Taylor, in his 2007 NEA Jazz Masters interview, recalls how Jones encouraged him not to drink, especially when playing piano: "Whiskey was the main narcotic of that particular time, and guys got drunk all the time and drank too much. Tatum, that's what killed him. But Jo tried his best to protect me from that. . . . I'm in college. You know, I'm a frat man. I'm hanging out with the guys on Saturday night. I could handle it, you know. But he knew I couldn't, and nobody could, really, under the circumstances that most of us worked in. . . . He came in and he had brought Teddy Wilson and Art Tatum in to hear me. Now I had been drinking. With both of them there, I'm nervous now. And because I had been drinking, I didn't feel that I was in control, you know, and I was embarrassed. . . . Never again. I said, 'Jo Jones, you made your point. I will never take another drink if I'm going to play the piano. I won't do that.' And that's what he did for me. I have to tell students this because, you know, here's a guy who was one of my elders who really did

that for me. . . . He drank and Tatum did, all those guys drank, you know, but they wouldn't let me do that." http://www.nea .gov.honors/jazz/jmCMS/master.php?id=1988_03&type=int (accessed January 17, 2010).

13. Madame Therese was Jones's friend for many years. Her full name, or real name, is unknown at this time. They had some type of serious relationship. She was from France and worked as a nurse at Mount Sinai Hospital in Manhattan. He says to Murray: "Madame Therese is my friend. Not my girlfriend. Not my woman. Not my wife. I have four rooms. It says Jonathan and Lorraine Jones." But Jones also says that Lorraine lives in California. He distinguishes her from his "first wife that died" (Jones told Milt Hinton her name was Vivien Greene and she was from Omaha). On one tape Jones says that at one point he had planned to marry Mabel Louise Smith, the singer known as Big Maybelle (1924–1972). According to Michael James, Madame Therese decided to return to France permanently and tried to convince Jones to join her, but he did not wish to leave the United States for good.

Madame Therese is mentioned briefly on many of the tapes. She is also mentioned in Preston Love's book *A Thousand Honey Creeks Later: My Life in Music from Basie to Motown* (Middletown, Conn.: Wesleyan University Press, 1997). According to Love, Jones visited Madame Therese in France for extended stays each year after she left New York. Jazz enthusiasts in France picked up the tab. Aside from Murray's work on *Good Morning Blues* during these years, this might help explain the 1982–85 gap in the Jones-Murray interviews. (The first draft of *Good Morning Blues* was finished in 1984. Meanwhile, Jones's health was failing.) Interestingly, Love claims that he and Jones were going to work on a Jones autobiography titled "Me and Count Basie." "What Jo Jones had to say about his association with Count Basie and his own career," Love writes, "should have been written down. It would have been interesting and edifying" (201). Understandably, Love was waiting for grant funds to materialize, and no content was ever created. See Phil Schaap's Afterword in this volume for more on Jones and other collaborators he turned to in the hope of completing his memoirs, including Love.

14. For more from Jones on the multitalented Kid Lips Hackett, see Korall, *Drummin' Men: The Swing Years,* 131–32 (originally published by Schirmer Books, 1990).

15. Jones often traveled to France to perform (that is, before he began going there in order to visit Madame Therese when his playing days were more or less over). Here he describes one trip of many, but it illustrates the extent to which he was appreciated in France.

16. He is referring to European state support of the arts.

THE COUNT BASIE INSTITUTION

1. Perhaps Jones is echoing Dan Morgenstern's claim in a 1966 liner note essay: "The Basie band is an institution, and institutions are often taken for granted—or criticized in non-institutional terms." See Morgenstern, *Living with Jazz,* 423. Then again, perhaps the echo runs the other way.

2. Compare with Captain Ahab in Herman Melville's *Moby Dick* (at the end of chapter 23): "for a whale-ship was my Yale College and my Harvard."

3. See Murray, *Good Morning Blues,* 149–50. For a similar but less specific version, see Bill Crow, *Jazz Anecdotes: Second Time Around* (New York: Oxford University Press, 2005), 58.

4. This anecdote was very important to Jones. It appears on almost every tape.

5. For Basie's take on the battle with Lunceford, see Murray, *Good Morning Blues,* 193–94.

6. This anecdote also appears on almost every tape. Basie "thought a lot of Charlie" and did him a big favor years later. See Murray, *Good Morning Blues,* 234.

7. This is somewhat unfair. Fletcher Henderson did help the band out by lending them some arrangements.

8. See John Hammond, *John Hammond on Record* (New York: Summit Press, 1977), 134. The Basie band was allowed to stay because the chorus girls loved to dance to Jones's beat.

Hammond notes that this was because Jones had been a dancer and knew how to play for dancers.

9. Hammond and Alexander were both white. Alexander (1908–1984) was Basie's booking agent through 1984.

10. When Jones says "socialite," he means someone who enjoys socializing or is very social. He does not mean "socialite" in the sense of someone in high society.

11. See Murray, *Good Morning Blues,* 235.

12. Catherine Morgan was a very sucessful dancer before marrying Count Basie.

13. The *Pittsburgh Courier,* a major black newspaper at the time, published these items by "Jule" in a gossip column called "The Talk O' Town" on February 13, 1937, p. 9: "Alice Dixon, pretty entertainer from the East, is in town with her Count Basie, who with his band, is the sensational attraction at the Chatterbox. . . . Alice is looking like a million dollars . . . and she and the Count are very much in love. . . . They are telling a good joke on the Count's appearance at the ofay spot. They say that one of those pretty young Nordic chicks came tripping into the Chatterbox to meet ROYALTY. 'I hear there is a real count here,' she chirped. Of course, Count Basie, a large, dark fellow was a complete surprise to her . . . and so was his enchanting music. I guess the little gal was looking for one of those Count No-Counts from Russia or sumpin'." This was published during the time in Pittsburgh when Jones punched the police officer. There is no mention of that in the archives of the *Pittsburgh Courier,* as Jones suggests there might be. The *Pittsburgh Courier* did cover the famous battle between Basie's band and Lunceford's band in Hartford, but the official archived article is so smudged as to be completely illegible.

14. Druid Hill Park is a park in Baltimore.

15. Murray interjects, "In that Washington orbit." Jones says, "Yeah!" Prominent African American families in and around Washington, D.C., were famously concerned with skin color, finding lighter skin more desirable.

16. Murray was also in the U.S. Army (Army Air Corps), from 1943 to 1946 and later on active duty in the U.S. Air Force from 1950

to 1962, retiring as a major in 1962. Jones was in the Army
from 1944 to 1946. Jones is asking the rhetorical question as
if anticipating Murray's question or anticipating that Murray
would have suspicion about the claim about phone access.

17. Several tunes were recorded on that date, February 4, 1946,
including "The King."

18. Jimmy Rushing, lead singer.

19. Murray lived on 132nd Street between 5th and Lenox Avenues.
Wilson Driver (1904–2000) was Jones's early drum teacher and
lifelong friend.

They Said the Negro Would Never Be Free

1. He means that not all of the white overseers were as mean as
Simon Legree, a character in *Uncle Tom's Cabin,* by Harriet
Beecher Stowe (1852).

2. Edgar Battle was a well-known jazz arranger.

3. Jumping, or jumping up and down, was slang for sex. Hence,
the title of one of Basie's best-known tunes, "Jumpin' at the
Woodside," is a triple entendre. It could be jumping as in
"the joint is jumping"; or lively, jumping as in dancing; or
jumping as in sex. The Woodside Hotel was a favorite spot
for dalliances with prostitutes. Jones often recalls the band
going up to the Woodside to "buy booty on credit." He recalls,
"We had women that would make a hundred-dollar call girl
look like shit. That's where 'Jumpin' at the Woodside' come
in." Another instance: "The girl said I owed her for six times.
I said, no, it was only five—that other boy, he looked like
me!" The incident described in this paragraph is described at
length and in detail in John Hammond's autobiography *John
Hammond on the Record,* 139–43. According to Dr. Arthur
Clinco, Jones's doctor at the Neurological Institute of New
York (cited by Hammond), marijuana plus secondary syphilis
is a combination that results in "an absolutely shattering blow
to the nervous system." Dr. Clinco went on to note that Jones
was not addicted to marijuana nor was marijuana an addictive
drug.

4. The Chatterbox was in the William Penn Hotel, the most prestigious hotel in Pittsburgh (known as the Omni William Penn in 2009, Jones tells Murray in 1978, "now it's the Penn-Sheraton"), and Basie's band was the first African American band to play there. In the little "Greek hotel" there must have been a lounge or bar where the incident that led to the police being called took place. Mayview is the Mayview Asylum for the Criminally Insane. If anything good came out of this incident, it is that Jones got his syphilis treated and became the first African American admitted at the Neurological Institute of New York. Also, the rest of the band was tested for syphilis, since they knew a lot of the same "ladies of the evening and what have you," and three ended up needing treatment. Syphilis has long been offered as an explanation for Jones's unusual mental state, but there is evidence that he was always a unique personality, and he would claim, "I was always a nut." However unusual his mental state was at times, he still served in the U.S. Army and received the Good Conduct Medal.

5. It is interesting and telling that Jones uses this story as an opportunity for insouciant signifyin'. In Hammond's maudlin and traumatized narration (after forty years), the story is taken very seriously (Hammond, *John Hammond on Record,* 139–43). Jones tells this story to Murray in a jovial mood, full of laughs as he adds an unexpected riff: the reason he was taken to the Mayview Asylum for the Criminally Insane is partially because he claimed that a *black* band was playing in the William Penn Hotel! As Jones would say: this is fast, man.

6. "I'm Mr. X" is said in the way a villain in a James Bond film might say it.

7. Boley, Oklahoma, was a black town founded in 1903. (It is still largely black today.) In 1932 Boley residents prevented a bank robbery attempt by George Birdwell, a close associate of Pretty Boy Floyd.

8. This could be an echo of a routine by the comedy team Stump and Stumpy, who often performed the Apollo Theater in the 1930s. They had a routine (which incorporated a repetition of the phrase "up N'oth") that juxtaposed expectations of life

in the North against its realities. See Lawrence W. Levine, *Black Culture and Black Consciousness: Afro American Folk Thought from Slavery to Freedom,* 30th Anniversary ed. (New York: Oxford University Press, 2007).

9. Billy Gladstone (1893–1961) was an influential drummer who performed at Radio City Music Hall for many years.

10. On the tape, Murray responds, "It's funny how Northern guys don't realize how we feel when we come up from Alabama after they've said all that stuff about what they're doing and what we were not doing, and yet you find that they're *more terrified,* you know, in so many instances!"

11. This famous hotel in Harlem was a destination for African American celebrities. Albert Murray has said that the bar scene at the Theresa in the late 1940s was something to behold. The hotel began to admit African Americans on a regular basis around 1940.

12. MCA was the Music Corporation of America, the largest booking agency of the time.

13. See Murray, *Good Morning Blues,* 252.

14. Vaudeville troupe Burnham, Harris, and Scott.

15. Robert Benjamin "Speck" Searcy (1901–1967) was mayor of Huntsville from 1952 to 1964.

16. I understand "it" to mean the Scottsboro incident itself, that Jones, then twenty years old, missed the train on which the black boys were accused of rape, so he almost became one of them. However, I have no confirmation of this interpretation.

17. On the tape, Murray laughs a little and asks in disbelief, "John Hammond was gonna make a quartet out of the Scottsboro Boys?" Jones replies, "Wellllll, it had been a big thing, you know." Murray: "Mmm-hmmm." Jones: "Had to do *something.*"

18. In this anecdote, Jones is apparently being harassed by a policeman in the same town where the Scottsboro trial is being held, but because he was so well known as a musician, the judge himself went out of his way to get him some food.

19. Jones attended Alabama A&M in Huntsville.

20. Alfred Steele (1901–1959) was the president of Pepsi-Cola from 1949 to 1959. He was married to Joan Crawford from 1955 to

1959. Long before this, Pepsi was one of the more progressive companies in the United States, employing many black salesmen.

My Thirst after Knowledge Will Never Cease

1. Elmer Simms Campbell (1906–1971) was an illustrator and cartoonist for *Esquire* and other magazines.
2. Either this list is not supposed to be in order, or he mixed up the order at the end. Jones met Murray before he met Ellison.
3. Jones is refering to Jervis Anderson's profile of Ralph Ellison, "Going to the Territory," in the *New Yorker,* November 22, 1976. Jones praises this outstanding profile in several conversations with Murray.
4. Herbert Asbury, *Gem of the Prairie: An Informal History of the Chicago Underworld* (New York: Alfred A. Knopf, 1940).
5. Ibid., 129. Murray read the quoted section onto the tape at Jones's request.
6. It is unclear where Jones came by this information.
7. Ibid., 257–58. Murray read this section onto the tape as well. Another section that Murray read is not included here because Jones did not comment on it. Pony Moore should not be confused with George Washington Moore, known as "Pony" (1815–1909), founder of Moore and Burgess's minstrels.
8. The source of this anecdote is unknown. It is delightfully reminiscent of *The Wizard of Oz.*
9. This was in 1955.
10. Compare with André Malraux's analogous distinction between the artist and the artisan in *The Voices of Silence* (Princeton, N.J.: Princeton University Press, 1978), 310: "I name that man an artist who creates forms, be he an ambassador like Rubens, an image-maker like Gislebert of Autun, a king's friend and court official like Velazquez, a rentier like Cezanne, a man possessed like Van Gogh or a vagabond like Gaugin; and I call that man an artisan who reproduces forms, however great may be the charm or sophistication of his craftsmanship." *The Voices of Silence* was first published in English in 1957 as *The*

Psychology of Art. In the documentary *Last of the Blue Devils* (1980), Count Basie makes a distinction between stylist and player similar to Jones's distinction but seems to lose his train of thought, while Jones's distinction is expressed with much more clarity and confidence, leading me to believe that Basie got the idea from Jones. It was more in character for Jones to theorize in such a way than it was for Basie.

11. Murray: "Cotton stalks!"

12. Sinclair Lewis (1885–1951) won the Nobel Prize for Literature in 1930. The source of the amusing and absurd claim Jones puts forth is unclear. From 1928 to 1940, Lewis was married to Dorothy Thompson, a prominent journalist. As for Shakespeare, it has been suggested on and off for several centuries that he had ghost writers or helpers or cowriters. This idea has been debunked but resurfaces every so often (most recently promulgated by U.S. Supreme Court Justice John Paul Stevens).

13. Thomas "Blind Tom" Wiggins (1849–1908) was an autistic pianist savant and composer, born into slavery and taken around the South to perform by his owner before the Civil War. He has since been the subject of several books.

14. Joel Augustus Rogers (1880–1966) was a prolific historian of African and African diasporic history. This is a rhetorical question of sorts.

15. Faith Baldwin (1893–1978) was a prolific romance novelist. Jones is making a joke at James Baldwin's expense. Murray's essay "James Baldwin, Protest Fiction, and the Blues Tradition" appeared in Murray's first book, *The Omni-Americans* (1970), and is critical of Baldwin.

16. The movie is *For Love of Ivy* (1968). Max Roach was married to Abby Lincoln at that time.

17. Usually when Jones refers to the "Invisible Man" he is referring to Ralph Ellison, author of the novel *Invisible Man*. He also refers to Ellison as Ralph, as he does earlier in this chapter. In this case, I believe Jones is referring to the novel, not Ellison.

18. Judging by the delivery and the tone, this question appears to be an echo of the scene in the film *The Philadelphia Story* (1940) in which C. K. Dexter Haven (Cary Grant) says to Macaulay Connor (Jimmy Stewart), "And you, a writer? Tsk. Tsk. Tsk.

I thought all writers drank to excess and beat their wives. You know, at one time I think I secretly wanted to be a writer."

19. Ellison started out as a trumpet player.

20. Murray riffs back to Jones: "The imitator is a kind of convenient bridge to the popular conception, the popular ability to understand. And then once that bridge is established, the better minds, the more serious people look for more and they go beyond that. That's more lasting when they get to it." Jones replies, "Oh, wait a second. Can I get you some, you know orange or some Coca-Cola or something, whatever?" Murray: "Yeah, orange juice, you got some orange juice?" Jones: "I think. I hope we don't run out."

21. Jones does not often allude to his current or former political beliefs, but this comment about Paul Robeson, shunned in the United States for a time for his Communist politics, may illuminate another statement Jones told to Murray. While Jones is showing old issues of *Downbeat* to Murray, he comes across a copy of *New Masses*. Jones: "*New Masses!* Now, some people said this was a Communist [publication]." Murray: "It was!" Jones: "Well, I don't know anything about that shit." According to Michael Denning, "Count Basie was part of a *New Masses* evening, Hitting a New High, in January 1938." Denning, *The Cultural Front: The Laboring of American Culture in the Twentieth Century* (New York: Verso, 1997), 334. If Jones read *New Masses* during its heyday in the 1930s, this is probably where he first encountered the writing of Ralph Ellison.

   Also, Paul Robeson recorded Richard Wright's blues "King Joe" (about Joe Louis) with the Basie band in 1941. For Basie's take on this recording, which was set up by John Hammond, see Murray, *Good Morning Blues,* 250–51. According to Basie, since Robeson had never sung the blues before, Jimmy Rushing coached him.

22. This is said with a very high degree of annoyance—such a sharp degree that Murray begins to laugh. Jones noted several times that he was a "printer by trade" or that printing was his trade. It is not clear where he learned the printing trade, but interestingly enough, Murray was a printer by trade himself. During the time Murray attended Tuskegee Institute (1935

to 1939), students were required to learn a manual trade in addition to any other course of study. Murray majored in education while also learning to be a printer.

23. James Monroe Trotter (1842–1892) escaped from slavery and became highly successful. *Music and Some Highly Musical People* (Boston and New York: Lee and Sheperd and Charles Dillingham, 1878) has been reprinted many times. Jones mentions it briefly on several tapes.

24. Jim and Andy's was a bar at Forty-eighth Street and Sixth Avenue in Manhattan that was popular with jazz musicians in the 1960s.

25. Toots Shor's was a famous bar/restaurant in midcentury Manhattan. The original venue was open from 1940 to 1959 and later opened again in other locations. Toots Shor's was known for attracting entertainers, athletes, journalists, politicians, and actors (for more, see the 2006 documentary *Toots.*) From the fact that Jones was there, it appears to have not been so cold toward African Americans as its competitor the Stork Club famously was. (The Stork Club is where Josephine Baker first met Grace Kelly, after Kelly stood up for her when she received poor service.) Frank Sinatra was a close friend of Toots Shor and a regular customer. It is impossible to conceive that he could countenance anything less than equal treatment. The connection between Jones and Toots Shor's may have been Jackie Gleason, who was (according to Milt Hinton) a regular at the Embers and also the customer perhaps most closely associated with Toots Shor's (see Hinton, Berger, and Maxson, *Playing the Changes,* 168).

26. The text in quotation marks is from an unknown article that Jones is reading aloud from onto the tape. Jones *seems* to be reading from a text, crinkling papers, saying, "it says here," and so on, generally purporting to quote a source. But those sentences are not like standard sports-page copy—they are more like Jo Jones. Isaac Burns Murphy was re-intered again some years later at the Kentucky Horse Park in Lexington. All the sources I've found use the term "Colored Archer" instead of "Dark Archer."

27. African Cemetary No. 2.

28. OTB is shorthand for off-track betting, a quasi-public chain of pari-mutuel wagering parlors, once ubiquitous in Manhattan and throughout New York State. The signs outside generally said "OTB."

29. Earl H. Sande (1898–1968), pronounced "sandy" by Jones, was a jockey and trainer, not to be confused with the jockey Earl "Sandy" Graham (1911–1927) who rode Seabiscuit. The scandal Jones is probably referring to is a prerace horse/jockey switcharoo that shocked the racing world. Despite that, Sande is one of the most highly regarded jockeys of all time. His blownup photograph hangs today alongside those of other horse racing notables above the teller windows on the ground floor at Belmont Park. Sande is mentioned briefly in *Invisible Man.*

30. In the 1960s and 1970s Jones was a partner with Frank Ippolito in a drum shop called Professional Percussion Center on Eighth Avenue and Fiftieth Street in Manhattan. The shop also sold other instruments, including guitars. The documentary *Born to Swing* (1973) includes scenes of Jones in the drum shop. One of Murray's tapes is labeled "Frank's Percussion Center, 12/24/77" and features Murray, Jones, and Frank Ippolito hanging out and talking for several hours while people come in and out of the drum shop.

31. A painting or drawing of his hands and sock cymbal.

PEOPLE I'VE RUBBED ELBOWS WITH

1. The section on Duke Ellington is the only section in *Rifftide* that was not told to Albert Murray personally. Jo Jones delivered this section as a talk to the Duke Ellington Society in 1976. Murray was in attendance and taped it. Nowhere does the tape or Jo Jones mention the Duke Ellington Society, but I learned of the talk and some of its details from Michael James (who was in attendance) before I heard Murray's tape. Hearing the lecture on tape after having heard Mike describe it several times was quite a pleasant surprise.

2. *Back to Back: Duke Ellington and Johnny Hodges Play the Blues* (1959). Jones plays drums on the album. Jones also plays drums on *Side by Side: Duke Ellington and Johnny Hodges* (1959).

3. The 1956 Newport Jazz Festival was a watershed moment in Ellington's career in which Jones participated with a newspaper that was *not* the *Chicago Tribune*. (The Duke Ellington Society audience got the joke.) The 1956 Newport Jazz Festival is the subject of the outstanding book *Backstory in Blue: Ellington at Newport '56* by John Fass Morton (New Brunswick, N.J.: Rutgers University Press, 2008). Albert Murray wrote to Ralph Ellison of the legendary performance and the recording of it: "They say the first ones to start cutting loose that night were not the groundlings but the native Newporters, who suddenly realized that they got some of that kind of blue in their blood too. You hear old Duke in there sic-ing that stuff on just as if it's all happening somewhere in a tobacco shed or corn likker joint, and there's that fancy fingering in there treeing squirrels and running rabbits all over 27 counties and choruses. And if that new suped-up rhythm section weren't enough in itself, there's old *Jo Jones* standing down there beating on the edge of the stage with a tightly rolled copy of the *Christian Science Monitor*!" (Ellison and Murray, *Trading Twelves,* 161). (The *Christian Science Monitor* is a nonreligious newspaper.) Ellington wrote of Jones: "Jo Jones was the driving force behind our big success at Newport in 1956, the man with a blueprint for a bouncing, boiling bash, the man in the pit with the git-wit-it git. Out of sight of the audience, in the pit in front of the bandstand, slapping a backbeat with a newspaper, talking to us, he prodded us into a *Go, Baby!* drive that developed into the rhythmic groove of the century, with Paul Gonsalves down front at the microphone." See Ellington, *Music Is My Mistress,* 241.

4. It is difficult to convey in print the energy of these words, and of the last paragraph in particular, as Jones takes off like a preacher wrapping up a rousing sermon. Cheers and shouts from the audience are audible, and powerful applause is heard at the end.

5. Small world: Murray's adoptive father, Hugh Murray, was a laborer who sometimes managed semipro baseball teams in Mobile, Alabama. Satchell Paige, who was from Mobile, pitched for Hugh Murray. Albert Murray grew up watching Paige.

6. My interpretation is that Jo had to keep the woman away from him because he would get out of hand when he drank.

7. Jones must mean *Zenobia* (1939), which featured Fetchit and McDaniels. Jones told Milt Hinton in his Jazz Oral History Project interview that he once filled in for Stepin Fetchit on a medicine show.

8. Jones is more excited and manic than usual when narrating this section about Fiddler.

9. Fritz Kreisler (1875–1962) and Jascha Heifetz (1901–1987) (whose real name was Joseph) were two of the most prominent violin players of the twentieth century. For many months, I thought Jones was referring to Fritz Crisler (1899–1982), the great college football coach. That did not make sense in the context until I found out about Fritz Kreisler. Herbert Orin Crisler was nicknamed "Fritz" after Fritz Kreisler by another legendary coach, Amos Alonzo Stagg. I am including this because Albert Murray loves old-time college football, and I have a feeling Jones would say HA!

10. Mr. Bregman is probably music publisher Jack Bregman.

11. Speaking of the beat, interestingly, Eddie Durham told Murray in a taped interview in January 1979, "I said Jo, *remember this tempo*. And he did! No other band had that tempo."

12. Lester Lanin (1907–2004) was a high society bandleader. I take Jones's comment about a "necessary evil" to mean that Lanin, while not being exactly artistically innovative, still gave a lot of work to musicians.

13. For Basie's take on the band's early association with Maceo Birch, see Murray, *Good Morning Blues,* 124.

14. St. Albans is a Queens, New York, neighborhood where many prominent jazz musicians settled. There is a well-known illustrated map of where they lived as well as a famous mural depicting many of them. Catherine and Count Basie Middle

School 72, a New York City public school, is located on Guy R. Brewer Boulevard, a few miles to the south of St. Albans.

15. Milt Ebbins (1912–2008) was a major show business impresario who managed top musicians and actors. This anecdote reflects Jones's distrust/dislike of white managers in that era, in the 1930s and 1940s.

16. Did he mean to say "talisman" when he said "Talmud"?

17. His full name was Love B. Woods. For more on him and the Theresa (and the Woodside, which he managed previously), see Sondra K. Wilson, *Meet Me at the Theresa: The Story of Harlem's Most Famous Hotel* (New York: Atria Books, 2004).

18. According to "Great Moments in Tuskgee University Athletics," "Tuskegee defeated Lincoln University of Pennsylvania 20–16 on Oct. 26 [1926] at the University of Pennsylvania's Franklin Field before 35,000 fans with All-American and College Football Hall of Famer Benjamin Stevenson scoring all of Tuskegee's points. 'Red' Grange, the thunder of the University of Illinois, was in the stands" (http://www.tuskegee.edu, accessed October 10, 2009).

19. Murray laughs heartily and says, "That's right!"

20. Polly Adler (1900–1962) was a famous madame. Her book, originally published by Rinehart in 1953, is *A House Is Not a Home* (Amherst: University of Massachussetts Press, 2006). There are a few references to people named "Louise" but it is unclear if they refer to Louise Kelly of Omaha. Omaha is mentioned once in passing. The connection between his foster mother and Polly Adler is not clear.

21. See notes for the chapter "They Said the Negro Would Never Be Free."

22. It is well known and well documented that John Hammond was liberal, trailblazing, and historically important in terms of helping to obtain equal treatment for blacks in the music business. Be that as it may, Jones has his own very strong feelings about Hammond. "R.P.P." was a label Jones used quite often. Meanwhile, Jones created various opportunities for non-black musicians, such as the pianist Dick Katz (1924–2009). Katz credited Jones with arranging for him to play (along with

Jones) on Benny Carter's album *Further Definitions* (1961). Katz also recalled an evening playing with Jones in a trio in a midtown Manhattan steakhouse in the 1950s. Jones defended Katz against a large group of white businessmen from Texas who were heckling Katz and asking him what he was doing up there with black musicians. Katz says that Jones snapped at them, with great authority, "He's playing the piano! What the hell do you think he's doing?" The hecklers backed off. Jones also mentored several white drummers (Jackie Mills, Shelly Manne, Chip Stern) as well as black drummers (J. C. Heard, Roy Haynes, Shelton Gary). For more on Jones and Mills, Manne, and Heard, see Burt Korall *Drummin' Men: The Heartbeat of Jazz; The Bebop Years* (New York: Oxford University Press, 2002).

I Often Wondered Why I Was Such a Strange Fella

1. Sugar Ray Robinson owned a restaurant in Harlem called Sugar Ray's.
2. Jones was a very good tennis player.
3. Occasionally Jones adopts an accent that is very close to what was once known as "Locust Valley lockjaw." This was the stereotypical accent, named for the enclave of Locust Valley on Long Island, of the upper classes around New York for most of the twentieth century. It found its way into popular culture via movies, television, and the speech of political figures, such as Franklin Delano Roosevelt. Jones probably had friends (John Hammond, at least) who spoke with this accent to one degree or another, and he might have associated it with, for example, an old and eminent professor.
4. Roscoe Conkling Simmons (1881–1951) was a prominent African American journalist and a famous orator. He was Booker T. Washington's nephew. (Washington's wife was sister to Simmons's mother.) After reading this section of text in 2006, Albert Murray recalled that he too had seen Roscoe Conkling Simmons speak (on the tape with Jones, Murray does not say anything). Murray was in attendance when Simmons spoke at the installation of Frederick Douglass Patterson (1901–1988) as

president of Tuskegee in 1935. In Murray's recollection, Simmons spoke after Mary McLeod Bethune, who Murray remembers saying, "Frederick Douglass Patterson: keep your hand on the plough!" Murray remembers Simmons speaking next and introducing a bit of complex Tuskegee humor into the occasion: Simmons recalled that, perhaps in "nineteen aught four," he worked as a laborer with the construction crew that built "this magnificent edifice" where the ceremony was taking place that day in 1935. Simmons described the hard manual labor in the hot sun as the building took shape. It was high-flying oratory, full of mighty rhetorical flourishes. Then, Simmons suddenly became colloquial, adding: "*And I never got my money!* I had to go see Uncle Booker and write to this person and that person— and I *never* got my money!" Murray told this story several times in 2006 and 2007 with much enthusiasm and affection.

5. 41603 Harlem is a gibberish address, which Jones is saying is imagined by someone who assumes he lives in Harlem. Jones lived on the Upper East Side. He did not actually live on Sutton Place (the street) but in Sutton Place the neighborhood/ area, and for a time in the East Sixties and also at 333 E. Fifty-fourth Street, where many of the tapes were recorded. (Some of the tapes were recorded at the West End and at Murray's apartment in Harlem.) In the 1950s Jones had a long-running gig (along with Marian McPartland and others) at the Embers, a posh club on the Upper East Side near where he lived. Jones also played for a time at the Embers with Joe Bushkin, Milt Hinton, and Buck Clayton. Hinton noted that the quartet represented three of the major big bands, with Bushkin (Tommy Dorsey), Jones and Clayton (Basie), and Hinton (Cab Calloway) (Hinton, Berger, and Maxson, *Playing the Changes,* 167). According to Benny Powell, the British political figure Lord Mountbatten (1900–1979) would make a point of catching Jones's performances there when he was in New York.

6. Hickey Freeman manufactured high-quality suits for men.

7. Matlaw's was an upscale men's clothing shop at the famous intersection of Eighteenth Street and Vine Street in Kansas City, a stone's throw from where the American Jazz Museum

is today on Eighteenth. "A cosmopolitan oasis, 18th and Vine became a cultural Mecca for African Americans from smaller burgs across the Midwest" (Frank Driggs and Chuck Hadix, *Kansas City Jazz: From Ragtime to Bebop—A History* [New York: Oxford University Press, 2006], 26).

8. Murray responds in the affirmative.

9. Willie Ruff is a French horn player and educator who taught for many decades at Yale University. He is from the Muscle Shoals region of Alabama, where Jones hoboed (in the vicinity of Decatur). Jones and Ruff were there for some reason, and someone from the old days said, "Jo, they cut your tree down." Albert Murray wrote the foreword to a book about Ruff, see William Zinnser, *Mitchell and Ruff: An American Profile in Jazz* (Philadelphia: Paul Dry Books, 2000; reprint of *Willie and Dwike,* first published in 1984).

10. Though he says "by a tree" in this instance, Murray has said that Jones sometimes said "up a tree" in nontaped conversation. Both are plausible. Perhaps it was "up a tree" during heavy rain when the ground was muddy. In Murray's novel *The Seven League Boots,* the character Joe States (based on Jo Jones—see the Introduction to this volume) says, "I'm talking about I'm the one that hit the trail out of Birmingham with my trap set in a goddamn cotton sack, and I'm talking about laboring on the L and goddamn N Railroad. And whenever I decided to stop off somewhere for a few days I'd hide my sack in the thickets down by the railroad until I found myself a little gig to pick up enough change to move on." See Murray, *The Seven League Boots,* 4.

11. This is said in an authorititative voice, like a judge handing down a sentence.

12. Compare this anecdote with the plot of *Great Expectations* by Charles Dickens, in which a young boy, Pip, brings some food to an escaped convict. The convict later makes a fortune in Australia and pays for Pip's education.

13. Ahmet Ertegun (1923–2006) was the founder of Atlantic Records, and Nesuhi Ertegun (1917–1989) was an executive there. Ahmet Ertegun was portrayed in the 2004 film *Ray.* The

Erteguns' father, Munir Ertegun, was Turkish ambassador to the United States from 1934 to 1944. The Nesuhi Ertegun Jazz Hall of Fame is a component of Jazz at Lincoln Center. Jones was inducted in 2005, the year after the Hall of Fame opened.

14. Billy Williams (1910–1972) was a singer. Sid Caesar and Imogene Coca were comedians who were on a comedy sketch television series called *Your Show of Shows* that ran from 1950 to 1954.

15. This possibly refers to jazz pianist Leslie Sheffield.

16. Lord Beaverbrook (William Maxwell Aitken) (1879–1964) was a newspaper mogul at the time Jones met him and later played a crucial role in the British war effort during World War II as one of Winston Churchill's cabinet ministers. Lord Beaverbrook was a self-made mogul and was originally from Canada. Jones spent some time in Canada in the 1920s. It is interesting that Jones mentions his meeting with Beaverbrook to Murray several times. Beaverbrook was well known for his dynamic and mischievous personality. Perhaps Jones saw something of himself in Beaverbrook.

17. Murray says, "You and I went through that. I was there!" Jones lapses into a pidgin French with his reply of "Perdu. OK?," as if to say, "Sorry, I forgot." This remains unclear. Perhaps Jones is imagining a future trip and forgot that Murray was on a past trip. Or was Murray at Tuskegee for some reason and just happened to run into Jones? (Murray left Tuskegee permanently in 1954, but he visited often and still had old friends there in 2011.)

18. Moton (1867–1940) was the second president of Tuskegee. Councill (1848–1909) was the founder of Alabama A&M.

19. Lillian Jordan, then of Englewood, New Jersey.

20. Jones attended junior high school with Haywood Henry in Birmingham. For Henry's interesting recollections of Jones (including Jones's prowess as a boxer), see Korall, *Drummin' Men: The Swing Years,* 130–31.

21. Jones is referencing *Uncle Tom's Cabin* by Harriet Beecher Stowe, chapter 20. Topsy, a character in *Uncle Tom's Cabin,* was "never born" but rather was "raised by a speculator, with

lots of others." Topsy continues, famously, "I 'spect I grow'd. Don't think nobody never made me." Jones mixes up the wording a little bit; for "just born" he probably meant to say "just growed." The joke here is that Jones does little to nothing to fill in the 1926 to 1934 gap that he talks about. Jones also uses this Topsy analogy with Milt Hinton and also does not provide him with much information on the period. There is some information about his pre-Basie life in Korall's *Drummin' Men: The Swing Years,* culled from interviews with him and others. Also, of course, Eddie Durham's composition "Topsy" was a 1937 hit for the Basie band and became a bigger hit in 1958 for Cozy Cole. Eddie Durham told Albert Murray about the origin of the composition in an interview in January 1979. Durham composed "Topsy" on a train to Albany, where he was to join the Basie band. Durham apparently did not have *Uncle Tom's Cabin* in mind when he named the piece, and neither he nor Murray brings up the book or character. He tells Murray that somebody else, while the composition was just completed and still in pencil, said, "Man, that's Topsy!" and that became the name. For Basie's take on Durham's rejoining Basie (who he'd played with in Moten's band) and bringing "Topsy" with him, see Murray, *Good Morning Blues,* 194.

22. He punctuated this with the sound of a loud "smack."

Index

Papa Jo Jones (1911–1985) was one of the most important drummers in the history of jazz and a driving force behind many innovations of the swing band era. As drummer for the Count Basie Orchestra beginning in 1936, he backed performers like Billie Holiday, Lester Young, and Herschel Evans. He played on landmark recordings throughout his career with Charles Mingus, Benny Carter, and Duke Ellington and appeared live with many prominent musicians, including Ella Fitzgerald and Teddy Wilson.

Albert Murray is the author of many works of fiction, nonfiction, and criticism, including *The Omni-Americans, South to a Very Old Place, Train Whistle Guitar, Stomping the Blues,* and *Good Morning Blues: The Autobiography of Count Basie as Told to Albert Murray.* A cofounder of Jazz at Lincoln Center, he graduated from Tuskegee Institute and taught at many colleges and universities.

Paul Devlin is a Ph.D. student in the English department at the State University of New York at Stony Brook. His writing has appeared in the *New York Times Book Review, Slate,* the *San Francisco Chronicle,* and other publications.

Phil Schaap has broadcast jazz on New York City's WKCR for more than forty years. He taught at Princeton University and currently teaches at Juilliard. He is the curator at Jazz at Lincoln Center.